CUSTOMER PILLARS

Nine foundational business building principles
which dictate the revenue and profitability
progress of every successful company

Curt Clinkinbeard

Strive Publishing
www.customerpillars.com

FIRST EDITION

Library of Congress Control Number: 2005911166

Clinkinbeard, Curt
    Customer Pillars – Nine foundational business building principles which dictate the revenue and profitability progress of every successful company / Curt Clinkinbeard. – 1st ed.

ISBN 978-0-9769064-2-1

1. Entrepreneurship. 2. Small Business – Management. 3. Success in Business. 4. Marketing

10   9   8   7   6   5   4   3

Copyediting: Kathy Foster
Page Layout: Digital Dragon Designery
Cover / Illustrations: Curt Clinkinbeard & Carl Masters
Author Photograph: Dan Mauer

The contents of this book should be considered management thoughts, suggestions, and insights, but do not abdicate the individual businessperson from making intelligent decisions for running their specific business in their specific industry. The goal of the book is to help the reader capitalize on opportunities, but does not reduce or eliminate the personal responsibility for decisions made in a business.

TABLE OF CONTENTS

AN OPEN LETTER TO READERS

Thank you for purchasing the **CUSTOMER PILLARS** Implementation Guide. This workbook will assist you with putting the *CUSTOMER PILLARS* system into action in your business. We wish you the best in growing your company.

As you probably know, in addition to this implementation guide, there is a standard book which explains the *CUSTOMER PILLARS* system. The two products work together; one (the book) explains a system. The other (this implementation guide) puts the concepts in motion in your individual business. There are pages listed in parentheses next to each of the exercises; these page numbers refer to the pages in the *CUSTOMER PILLARS* book where the concept is explained in more detail. Use the book and the implementation guide together.

There are several things to consider when working on this guide:

First, avoid the temptation to answer the questions only at a surface level. Many of the questions can be answered with quick and short answers. However, this shortchanges the exercise. The goal is to look at these questions at a deep level, with specifics and details, under the microscope. Often the best business development nuggets are found beneath the surface. Dig around in these topics a bit. Don't be in a rush. Better to do one exercise with strong consideration than to hurry through ten of them.

The workbook is not really intended to be a stand alone product. The concepts behind the questions are not explained in great deal. Use the book or a consultant to assist you with understanding the concepts. The implementation guide is mostly about how the concepts apply to you and giving you a place to brainstorm and collect your ideas.

Don't be overwhelmed if this seems like a lot of material. It is. So long as you are in business, you will be considering these items and improvements to them. It is not something you finish. It is an ongoing process.

Another thing: do not feel that you need to start at the beginning of the implementation guide and go through it question by question. Feel free to peruse the exercises and start with the ones you feel will benefit you the most. Go ahead and look for "low hanging fruit" or things you feel will produce the most immediate impact.

I wish you much success in learning and taking the principles found within and putting them into your business. Getting really good at what is found in this implementation guide has many handsome rewards. To the extent your business will make your dreams come true, it will do so within the context of these theories and the exercises found herein.

I want your business to reach the goals you have for it.

Please feel free to contact the author at curt@strivecoaching.com to make comments, suggestions, or observations – including complaints! Additionally, the *CUSTOMER PILLARS* website features many free downloadable tools relating to the book, as well as other products and services to assist you with your expansion effort.

If you like the book and it helps you, please tell a friend. Even better, send me a testimonial email. Positive reader feedback is extremely helpful! The greatest compliment you can provide me is to encourage others to use this guide as well.

The *CUSTOMER PILLARS* system is designed to help you and your business reach your potential. Go do it!

Please visit our website at:

WWW.CUSTOMERPILLARS.COM

INTRODUCTION

INTRODUCING THE *CUSTOMER PILLARS*

INTRODUCING THE *CUSTOMER PILLARS*

GOALS OF THE *CUSTOMER PILLARS* SYSTEM

- Increase customer revenues and profitability – improve the outputs / rewards you get from your business

- Improve the enjoyment of owning or managing a business

- Thoroughly understand and execute the basics – these are what drive the success of companies

Question: Imagine you become **really** good at building profitable revenues in your business. What would this mean to your company and to you personally? Describe what it would be like if you could grow good quality revenues *at will*. (pp 3 - 4)

**CONSIDER THE BENEFITS OF BEING
REALLY GOOD AT BUILDING YOUR BUSINESS**

Key Assumptions of the *CUSTOMER PILLARS* System

- Keeping costs under control is a vital management component, but many small businesses have already cut costs about as much as they can – most small companies are not "fat and happy"

- To improve the performance of the business, good quality revenues must increase

- Nearly every business has an incredible amount of growth potential

Discuss ten points to describe good quality revenues and contrast this to ten points that describe revenues of lesser quality. (pp 14 – 17)

Good Quality Revenues	Lesser Quality Revenues

PAY ATTENTION TO THE QUALITY OF YOUR GROWTH

The *CUSTOMER PILLARS* system is organized around nine naturally occurring principles – these pillars (a) apply to every company, (b) are wide in their scope, (c) are continually evolving in a company, and thus, (d) require ongoing management and improvement. The nine pillars are:

THE 9 *CUSTOMER PILLARS*

Pillar 1   Focus on Growth Customers

Pillar 2   Maximize Value Incrementally

Pillar 3   Refine Toward Perfect Pricing

Pillar 4   Form Productive Linking Relationships

Pillar 5   Sharpen Your Competitive Edge

Pillar 6   Connect Powerfully with Customers

Pillar 7   Manage Expectations Brilliantly

Pillar 8   Learn from the Market

Pillar 9   Practice Coordinated Growth Planning

Here is a brief overview of each pillar: (pp 4 - 8)

PILLAR 1: FOCUS ON GROWTH CUSTOMERS

This concept recognizes that to increase good quality revenues and profits, the company must focus on those who will contribute to that growth: the customers. The pillar asks the company to emphasize the customer, know the customer and their needs at a deeper level, and to develop a customer orientation throughout their entire company.

Based on your initial impression, would you rate this as a strength or a weakness in your company?   _____ Strength   _____ Weakness

Explain how this pillar might impact your company.

PILLAR 2: MAXIMIZE VALUE INCREMENTALLY

Customers purchase from companies because their products or services produce value for them. Too often we think about what our products and services ARE, but in reality, customers buy them for what they DO for them. It's a subtle, but important shift. This fundamental asks you to consider ways you can continually improve the value you produce for customers. This helps you advance!

Based on your initial impression, would you rate this as a strength or a weakness in your company?   ____ Strength   ____ Weakness

Explain how this pillar might impact your company.

PILLAR 3: REFINE TOWARD PERFECT PRICING

The price you charge customers has a significant effect on your relationship with customers, but also has a dramatic impact on the financial results of the company. Pricing is often a challenging topic. The theory suggests you refine your pricing to a more ideal level.

Based on your initial impression, would you rate this as a strength or a weakness in your company?   ____ Strength   ____ Weakness

Explain how this pillar might impact your company.

PILLAR 4: FORM PRODUCTIVE LINKING RELATIONSHIPS

Linking relationships – referral partners, distribution partners, strategic alliances, and key influencers – are important associations that link customers to your company. These companies or individuals are significant to expanding the business and can be one of the most important approaches to building your company.

Based on your initial impression, would you rate this as a strength or a weakness in your company?   ____ Strength   ____ Weakness

Explain how this pillar might impact your company.

PILLAR 5: SHARPEN YOUR COMPETITIVE EDGE

Every company operates in a competitive environment. This principle helps you distinguish yourself from similar companies and helps customers answer the question "Why should I purchase from you instead of from other competitors?". Sharpening your competitive edge is an important part of the development process.

Based on your initial impression, would you rate this as a strength or a weakness in your company?   ____ Strength   ____ Weakness

Explain how this pillar might impact your company.

PILLAR 6: CONNECT POWERFULLY WITH CUSTOMERS

Communicating with customers helps educate them about your business and why they should be interested in your firm. Connecting the gap between what customers know and think about you and what you would like them to know and think about you is the goal of this principle.

Based on your initial impression, would you rate this as a strength or a weakness in your company?   _____ Strength   _____ Weakness

Explain how this pillar might impact your company.

PILLAR 7: MANAGE EXPECTATIONS BRILLIANTLY

Customers enter every transaction with expectations about how the company will perform. Exceed those expectations and customers will think your company is great and will lead to significant benefits. If the customer believes you perform under their expectations, they will be disappointed. How well you do here ultimately determines your business success.

Based on your initial impression, would you rate this as a strength or a weakness in your company?   _____ Strength   _____ Weakness

Explain how this pillar might impact your company.

PILLAR 8: LEARN FROM THE MARKET

Figuring out customers is no easy task and the assumptions we make about them has a significant impact on our results. So, the more we learn about and from customers, the better. Evolving companies use testing and research processes to better understand their customers. Adapting and modifying your approach based on new knowledge is a foundation of growth.

Based on your initial impression, would you rate this as a strength or a weakness in your company?   ____ Strength   ____ Weakness

Explain how this pillar might impact your company.

PILLAR 9: PRACTICE COORDINATED GROWTH PLANNING

Pulling together all of the business expansion initiatives into a coordinated, written plan is an important part of the business development process. Good planning looks not only at how to build the business, but on the impact revenue growth will have on the entire company, as well as the tactical implementation necessary to carry out the plan.

Based on your initial impression, would you rate this as a strength or a weakness in your company?   ____ Strength   ____ Weakness

Explain how this pillar might impact your company.

OBSERVE YOUR FIRST IMPRESSIONS TO THE PILLARS

We look at a couple of ratios to gauge the growth progress of the company. The growth efficiency ratio tells us how effective the company has been in converting revenue increases into profitability increases. (pp 14 - 16)

Growth Efficiency Ratio = % Change in Profits ÷ % Change in Revenues

	Period 1	Period 2	Period 3	Period 4	Period 5
Date Range					
Revenues					
Net Profit					
% CH in Revenues	n/a				
% CH in Profits	n/a				
Growth Efficiency Ratio	n/a				

Date Range = The amount of time covered in each of the periods (for instance year, quarter or month), start earlier and progress later
Revenues = Total sales revenues for the time period
Net Profit = Bottom line profits
% Ch in Revenues = For Period 2 = (Revenues Period 2 – Revenues Period 1) / Revenues Period 1
% Ch in Profits = For Period 2 = (Profits Period 2 – Profits Period 1) / Profits Period 1
Growth Efficiency Ratio = % CH in Profits / % CH in Revenues

What does the growth efficiency ratio tell you about what is going on inside of your company?

CALCULATE YOUR GROWTH EFFICIENCY RATIO

	Industry Growth Ratio = Company's Annual Growth % ÷ Industry Growth %.

The Industry Growth Ratio compares the company's growth with the overall growth in the industry. This compares how rapidly you are advancing in relation to your industry. Additionally, this tells you if you are gaining or losing market share. (pp 16 - 17)

	Year 1	Year 2	Year 3	Year 4	Year 5
Year					
Revenues					
% CH in Revenues	n/a				
Average Industry Growth Rate					
Industry Growth Ratio					

Revenues = Total sales revenues for the time period
% Ch in Revenues = For Year 2 = (Revenues Year 2 – Revenues Year 1) / Revenues Year 1
Industry Growth Ratio = % CH in Revenues / Average Industry Growth Ratio

What does the industry growth ratio tell you about what is going on inside your company?

COMPARE YOUR GROWTH TO THE INDUSTRY

You can learn a great deal about growing a company by watching firms in other industries. Quite often some of the best expansion strategies are when a firm observes a strategy in another industry, then brings it to their own. Be on the lookout for these observations and record them here: (pp 13 - 14)

Company / Industry	Their Growth Strategy	How Can You Apply This to Your Industry?

LEARN FROM OTHER INDUSTRIES

What are your expansion goals? (pp 17)

Overall	In 1 Year	In 3 Years	In 10 Years

What will achieving these goals mean to your business?

What will achieving these goals mean to you personally?

BE SPECIFIC ABOUT YOUR EXPANSION GOALS

How do you need to grow personally (learn, develop, change) as a business manager to accomplish these goals?

YOUR GROWTH WILL DRIVE YOUR COMPANY'S GROWTH

Employees or members of your team who "get" the principles behind the *CUSTOMER PILLARS* system are much more likely to contribute to the expansion goals of the company. List ten steps you could take to ensure your team learns these principles as well.

1.

2.

3.

4.

5.

6.

7.

8.

9.

10.

TEACH EMPLOYEES THIS DEVELOPMENT SYSTEM

Growth is a mindset. List ten ways you can instill a growth mindset in yourself and in others in your company. (pp 17)

1.

2.

3.

4.

5.

6.

7.

8.

9.

10.

GROWTH IS A MINDSET

PILLAR 1

FOCUS ON GROWTH CUSTOMERS

PILLAR 1: FOCUS ON GROWTH CUSTOMERS

This pillar recognizes that your growth comes from customers, thus emphasizing, understanding, and catering to specific customer's needs is imperative. The broader you define your customer groups, the more difficult it is to specifically understand those customers and their individual needs. Thus, an important part of the *CUSTOMER PILLARS* process is to segment your customer base so you can study their specific traits.

Divide your customers into segments, list key characteristics of each, discuss the current revenue "mix," as well as your ideal mix. (pp 22 - 24)

Customer Segment	5 Key Characteristics	Existing % of Revenue	Targeted % of Revenue
1.			
2.			
3.			
4.			
5.			
6.			

SEGMENT YOUR CUSTOMER BASE INTO KEY GROUPS SO YOU CAN BE MORE SPECIFIC ABOUT UNDERSTANDING THEM. UNDERSTAND YOUR MIX BETWEEN THESE GROUPS

Another way to segment customers is based on 3 kinds of customers every company sells to: (1) current customers, (2) previous customers, and (3) new customers. List the top five things you are doing now to develop revenues with each of these categories, as well as seven things you could do with each segment to prompt additional revenues. (pp 24 - 37)

Present Activities Current Customers	Previous Customers	New Customers

Possible / Future Activities Current Customers	Previous Customers	New Customers

BREAK CUSTOMER APPROACHES INTO 3 GROUPS: CURRENT, PREVIOUS, AND NEW CUSTOMERS

Retaining current customers is a strong revenue strategy. Once customers come into our business, we want them to stay and to buy more. List the top ten reasons why customers would repurchase from your company. (pp 24 - 30)

STUDY THE REASONS CUSTOMERS COME BACK TO YOUR BUSINESS

Assume the bank comes to you and mandates that you DOUBLE your revenues only by selling more to your existing customers. If you are not successful, they will pull your loan and you will have to close the business. List ten steps you would take to double revenues selling to only your existing customer base: (pp 24 - 30)

IDENTIFY KEY WAYS TO INCREASE REVENUES
BY SELLING TO YOUR EXISTING CUSTOMER BASE

When studying your current customers, it is often valuable to make some calculations (pp 24–28)

A. Take an annual level of your sales	
B. Number of customers you sold to during that year	
C. Average annual customer purchase (Divide A by B)	
D. List the average customer potential per year (how much could you sell to each)	
E. If customers were to buy from you for their lifetime, on average, how many years would that be?	
F. Calculate the lifetime value of the customers (Multiply D times E)	
H. Calculate your current share of customer (Divide C by D)	

(Note: It is valuable to conduct this analysis for your key customer segments individually, as well as studying these numbers on an overall basis.)

What observations can you make about your business based on the lifetime value of the customer? What opportunities for expansion exist here? (pp 24 - 28)

CALCULATE THE LIFETIME VALUE OF YOUR CUSTOMER

What observations can you make about your business based on the share of customer calculation? What opportunities for advancement exist here? Do you see ways to increase the average amount a customer purchases from your business? (pp 24 - 28)

CALCULATE THE SHARE OF CUSTOMER YOU CURRENTLY CONTROL

In the "three customers every company sells to" analysis, the second group to consider is previous customers. Reactivating those who once purchased from you, but have not in some time, is often a successful and efficient strategy.

Discuss five ways you could effectively identify previous customers who are most likely to purchase again from your company? (pp 30 - 33)

1.

2.

3.

4.

5.

Describe how you can (or could) use your customer database to help with this process?

HAVE METHODS TO IDENTIFY PREVIOUS CUSTOMERS

List five things you could say to previous customers in re-contacting them to invite them back to your business. (pp 30 - 33)

1.

2.

3.

4.

5.

DEVELOP LANGUAGE TO INVITE CUSTOMERS BACK TO YOUR BUSINESS

List four things you can do in the short-term in your business to reactivate previous customers and have a significant impact on your revenues. For each list three action steps you need to take to ensure this happens.(pp 30 - 33)

4 Things to Reactivate Previous Customers	3 Action Steps for Each
	* * *
	* * *
	* * *
	* * *

REACTIVATE PREVIOUS CUSTOMERS AS AN EFFICIENT GROWTH STRATEGY

The third strategy when evaluating "three customers every company sells to" is to acquire new customers. Before venturing out into completely new strategies (which is risky) to get new customers, it makes sense to revisit some of the strategies that have been successful in the past at obtaining new customers. List five strategies that have been successful for getting new customers and three ways for each strategy you could expand and better leverage that approach (pp 34 - 37)

5 New Customer Strategies You Have Used Successfully in the Past	3 Ways to Expand / Further Leverage Each
	* * *
	* * *
	* * *

	* * *
	* * *

START NEW CUSTOMER EFFORTS BY STUDYING WHAT HAS ALREADY WORKED AND IDENTIFYING WAYS TO BETTER USE THESE SUCCESSFUL APPROACHES

In searching for new customers, the more specific we are about those customers, the more likely we are to develop appropriate strategies to bring them into our business. It's not good enough to just want new customers. Being specific about it is similar to the "ask and you shall receive" concept.

For Each Major Customer Segment, Describe Three Different Ideal Customer Prospects (Describe them in detail.) (pp 34 - 37)

For Each Major Customer Segment, Describe Three Different Ideal Customer Prospects (Describe them in detail.) (exercise continued)

BE SPECIFIC WHEN DESCRIBING THE NEW CUSTOMERS YOU SEEK

Until proven, new customer strategies are just tests – and you should treat them that way. List the top five new ways you are considering using to attract new customers. Next to each, list three ways you could test that approach: (pp 34 - 37)

5 New Customer Strategies	Three Ways to Test Each
	* * *
	* * *
	* * *
	* * *
	* * *

TREAT UNPROVEN NEW CUSTOMER STRATEGIES AS EXPERIMENTS UNTIL YOU CAN DOCUMENT SUCCESS

Identify ten people in your industry who are successful. Study their approaches to new customer development. If you are not competitors, call and interview them. Also, consider joining a mastermind or industry marketing group. After doing this research, list ten strategies others in your industry are using to gain new customers. (pp 34 - 37)

List Ten Strategies Others in Your Industry Are Using to Gain New Customers	Describe How You Could Use This Strategy in Your Business to Gain New Customers

STUDY SUCCESSFUL INDUSTRY "BEST PRACTICES" REGARDING NEW CUSTOMER ACQUISITION TO IDENTIFY POSSIBLE SOLUTIONS

Part of focusing on growth customers is to understand them very deeply. Part of this is realizing that customers buy to fill certain gaps in their lives or in their business. Thus, it is important to identify the "unmet needs" which motivate your customers to purchase from you. List five unmet customer needs and how you help fill those needs: (pp 38 – 40)

Unmet Customer Needs	How We Meet / Fill Them

FILL UNMET NEEDS

If you sell to consumers, ultimately the reasons motivating their purchase will track back to the fact that in some way your product improves the quality of their life. In selling to businesses, every purchase can ultimately be tracked back to the impact it will have on the company's profitability, financial health, or return on investment. These are called root emotional drivers. Start with customer drivers at the surface level and walk through the progression of drivers until you get to the root emotional drivers. (pp 38 - 40)

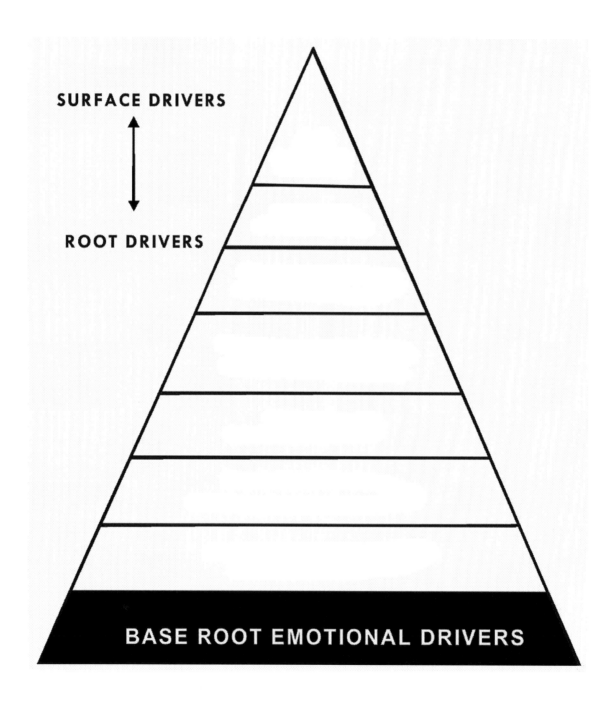

If you sell to consumers, every purchase must track back to one root buying emotion: that the purchase will ultimately improve their quality of life. What are five ways your product or service does this? (pp 38 - 40)

1.

2.

3.

4.

5.

IF YOU SELL TO CONSUMERS YOU MUST ADDRESS HOW YOUR PRODUCT OR SERVICE IMPROVES THE QUALITY OF THEIR LIVES

If you sell to businesses, every purchase must track back to one root buying emotion: that the purchase will ultimately improve the financial health of their company. What are five ways your product or service positively impact the financial health (profitability, return on investment, longevity, etc) of your customers? (pp 38 - 40)

1.

2.

3.

4.

5.

IF YOU SELL TO COMPANIES, YOU MUST ADDRESS HOW YOU IMPROVE THE FINANCIAL HEALTH OF THAT CUSTOMER

How do you incorporate these thoughts around these root buying emotions in the way you interact and communicate with customers? (pp 38 - 40)

USE ROOT DRIVING EMOTIONS WHEN COMMUNICATING WITH CUSTOMERS

Human motivation is often described in terms of "towards" or "away from" motives. In other words, people are either motivated to move toward positive outcomes or are driven to avoid negative circumstances. Please list six "towards" motivating factors and six "away from" motivating factors. (pp 40 - 41)

"Towards" Motivating Factors	"Away From" Motivating Factors

CUSTOMERS ARE MOTIVATED BY BOTH "TOWARDS" AND "AWAY FROM" FACTORS

What are seven things that your customers fear? What do you do to dissuade those fears? (pp 40 - 42)

Key Customer Fears	Actions to Minimize Customer Fears

UNDERSTAND YOUR CUSTOMERS' FEARS

One very common fear is where the client fears the transaction will somehow not live up to their expectations. How do you reduce this fear so the customer feels very comfortable doing business with you? How can you use warranties, guarantees, etc to your advantage? Use the following list to spark your creativity. (pp 41 - 42)

WAYS TO REDUCE CUSTOMER FEARS

- Money back / satisfaction guarantees

- Favorable, convenient return policies

- Warranties

- Quality statements / standards

- Sampling programs / free trials

- Testimonials

- Customer forums

- Make contact information very visible

TAKE ACTIONS TO REDUCE YOUR CUSTOMER'S FEARS THAT YOU WILL NOT LIVE UP TO YOUR PROMISES IN THE TRANSACTION

"Focusing on growth customers" should be an organizational priority – not just the job of the owner or the marketing department. What are ten steps you can take to ensure this is the emphasis of everyone in the company?

1.

2.

3.

4.

5.

6.

7.

8.

9.

10.

FOCUSING ON GROWTH CUSTOMERS SHOULD BE THE AIM OF EVERYONE IN YOUR COMPANY

Describe ten ways that "focusing on growth customers" will help propel your company forward. What did you learn / ideas did you generate from studying this pillar?

1.

2.

3.

4.

5.

6.

7.

8.

9.

10.

FOCUS ON GROWTH CUSTOMERS

PILLAR 2

MAXIMIZE VALUE INCREMENTALLY

PILLAR 2: MAXIMIZE VALUE INCREMENTALLY

Customers enter into transactions with your company not because of what you are selling, but based on what they think they will get out of it. This pillar suggests a change of emphasis away from products and services to an emphasis on creating real value for your customers and continuing to improve. There are multiple ways to do this including innovation, value added, bundling and packaging, and intellectual property. To receive, you often have to give first.

> Value = What the customer receives ÷ What the customer sacrifices

What are the seven most important things your customers get out of purchasing from your company? What are the key value points customers gain from your products or services? (pp 45 - 48)

1.

2.

3.

4.

5.

6.

7.

UNDERSTAND WHAT YOUR CUSTOMERS GET OUT OF PURCHASES FROM YOUR COMPANY

Describe how your customers view what they sacrifice to purchase from your company in relation to what they get out of it. Is this a good deal for them? WHY? (pp 45 - 47)

CUSTOMERS JUDGE WHAT THEY GET IN RELATION TO WHAT THEY SACRIFICE — THIS IS CALLED VALUE

List five things you could do to improve the ratio of what the customer gets from purchasing from you in relation to what they perceive they sacrifice. How do you make these things (a) possible, and (b) powerful for increasing your revenues? (pp 45 - 50)

1.

2.

3.

4.

5.

ALWAYS LOOK FOR WAYS TO INCREASE THE VALUE YOU PROVIDE TO CUSTOMERS. SUCCESSFUL COMPANIES DO THIS <u>AND</u> INCREASE PROFITS

We are usually very biased in the way we look at our own products and service. This "creation bias" can cloud our perception of how others (customers) view our offering. List ten ways your customer might perceive your value as less than you and your employees do. By each, list how you might change your marketing efforts based on this. (pp 48)

10 Ways Customers May Look at Our Products Less Favorably Than We Do	How Might You Change Your Approach to the Market Based on This?

CONSIDER HOW CREATION BIAS MAY BE CLOUDING YOUR VISION OF HOW CUSTOMERS LOOK AT YOUR COMPANY

This pillar suggests to "maximize value incrementally" which infers continuous and ongoing improvement in the value you bring to customers. What are five steps you could take to ensure you have an ongoing, long-term commitment to always improving the value you produce for customers? (pp 60)

1.

2.

3.

4.

5.

COMMIT TO INCREMENTAL AND ONGOING IMPROVEMENTS TO THE VALUE YOU CREATE FOR CUSTOMERS

Value-added is a strategy which attempts to add "little things that mean a lot" to your offering. Often these items add little or no cost to the products or services you offer, yet they significantly change the perception of value customers get from it. List ten ways you could use a "value-added" strategy. Next to each, list the estimated cost of adding this item, as well as how the customer's perception of value would improve: (pp 49)

List 10 Value-Added Strategies	List the Estimated Incremental Costs	How Would this Change Customer Perceptions?

LOOK FOR WAYS TO ADD VALUE TO YOUR OFFERING THAT ADD SIGNIFICANTLY TO CUSTOMERS' PERCEIVED VALUE, BUT ADD RELATIVELY LITTLE TO THE COST

Some companies employ a "one stop shop" approach to their product and service offering. What are seven products or services that you do NOT currently offer, but that your current customers may expect to purchase from a business like yours? Next to each, list (a) the estimated cost to add that product or service, (b) the estimated impact on revenues, and (c) the possible risks associated with this line extension. (pp 50 – 54)

Possible Line Extensions	Estimated Cost to Add to Line	Estimated Revenue Impact	Possible Associated Risks

CONSIDER LINE EXTENSIONS, BUT CAREFULLY STUDY THE POTENTIAL RISKS BEFORE TAKING ACTION

Often when we add new products or services to our line, base products shrink as the new products increase. What steps can you take to ensure new products do not cannibalize your existing products or services? (pp 51 – 52)

ENSURE NEW PRODUCTS RESULT IN INCREMENTAL REVENUE INCREASES, NOT JUST SHIFTING SALES FROM OLD PRODUCTS TO NEW ONES

Bundling products or services can be a great way to increase value, as well as increase the average order size from customers. One interesting bundling strategy would be to add products to a service offering or adding services to a product. What are five major bundling approaches you could take that would add value for your customers? (pp 52 – 54)

1.

2.

3.

4.

5.

BUNDLING OFFERS A SIGNIFICANT OPPORTUNITY TO ADD VALUE

Often product or service lines are structured so that the relationship can start with a simple, inexpensive, or narrow initial product or service, yet expand greatly through cross-selling or up-selling as the relationship deepens. Describe how your company could structure your product or service offering to tap into this progression of your offering (the back end) and lead the customer down a path of an increasing commitment to your company. (pp 52 - 54)

OFTEN CUSTOMER RELATIONSHIPS START SMALL AND DEVELOP OVER THE COURSE OF TIME - DESIGN YOUR OFFERING TO CAPITALIZE ON THIS

How does innovation impact your business regarding the products or services you offer? What are three innovations you could work on in the next few years that would significantly improve your approach to customers? (Use the table on the next page that lists the different types of innovation to spark some ideas.) (pp 55 – 56)

1.

2.

3.

LOOK FOR WAYS TO INNOVATE AND BRING UNIQUE SOLUTIONS / IMPROVEMENTS TO YOUR CUSTOMERS

Type of Innovation	Description	Example
Customer driven	Listening to the market and reacting to customer requirements	When a new law greatly impacts its clients, a law firm develops a program that meets customers' new needs
Service driven	Prompted by improvements in the ease or pleasure associated with doing business with your company	A coffee shop owner sees that people are bored while they wait, so she creates an interesting waiting area and a system to bring the coffees to customers there
Research driven	Using advances in technology / science to bring solutions to the marketplace	A medical firm partners with a university technology transfer department to commercialize products based on the school's research
Competitive driven	Development in reaction to the actions of competitors	When one sports bar succeeds with a Monday night special, the competition executes a similar strategy
Competency driven	Based on the internal skills of the company	A manufacturing firm has engineers with specialized skills that apply, not only to the current products they offer, but also to other areas; the company has the engineers explore these areas as well
Overhead driven	Development that leverages into previous expenditures from the company, for instance, a piece of equipment	A manufacturing firm purchases a welding machine, then finds other firms in different industries and subcontracts some of the welding work to them
By-products / waste driven	Often the process of producing a product or service produces by-products or waste that can be marketed and sold with a bit of creativity	A manufacturing firm cuts large pieces from metal sheets – to use the wasted scrap metal, they design new products that can be cut from the scrap without additional cost

Packaging can significantly shift the perception of value associated with your products (and even with services!). How does packaging impact your company? What are five packaging strategies you could utilize that would differentiate your company from others? (pp 56)

1.

2.

3.

4.

5.

USE PACKAGING AS A METHOD TO ADD VALUE TO YOUR PRODUCTS OR SERVICES

Similarly, branding can impact the customers' perception of value. How strong is your branding approach? What could you do to establish a significantly stronger brand in your industry which would produce great value for your company? (pp 56)

USE BRANDING AS A STRATEGY TO INCREASE VALUE

Are there ways that intellectual property (patents, trademarks, and copyrights) could significantly increase the perceived value of your products or services and protect the advantages your innovations create? Describe how these impact your business. (pp 56 - 57)

Patents	Trademarks	Copyrights

USE INTELLECTUAL PROPERTY AS A WAY TO INCREASE PERCIEVED VALUE AND PROTECT THE INNOVATIONS YOU CREATE FOR THE MARKET

Some product or services are a one-time sale and leave little opportunity to develop an ongoing revenue relationship with the company. This can be fairly limiting. Given it is expensive and difficult to develop customer relationships, we would like to leverage them over the long-term. Describe how your line is structured to develop a long-term, "residual stream" of revenues from your customers. How can you improve this? (pp 59 – 60)

DEVELOP YOUR PRODUCT LINE TO BE ABLE TO SELL TO THE CUSTOMER ON AN ONGOING, LONG-TERM BASIS. IF YOU HAVE A "ONE-TIME" SALE, LOOK FOR CREATIVE WAYS TO EXPAND THE RELATIONSHIP

What are the top seven key quality parameters your customers are judging you on? How would you judge yourself of each? What are quality improvements you could make that would have the most impact on customers? (pp 57)

Important Quality Parameters	Rate Your Current Performance	How Could You Improve?

UNDERTAND WHICH QUALITY PARAMETERS ARE IMPORTANT TO YOUR CUSTOMERS AND HOW YOU CAN IMPROVE IN THOSE AREAS

Are there assets in your marketing arsenal that you may consider licensing to others? How might you be able to license products, services, or brands from others to greatly increase your offering? Describe how you could capitalize on these opportunities. (pp 60)

USE LICENSING AS A VALUE ENHANCING STRATEGY

What are the key gaps that exist in your product or service offering? What could you do to profitably fill those holes? (pp 58)

**STUDY THE GAPS IN YOUR OFFERING
AND FIND PROFITABLE WAYS TO FILL THEM**

List ten ways the value your products and services produce for your customers can significantly improve teamwork, pride, and morale within your company. (pp 57)

1.

2.

3.

4.

5.

6.

7.

8.

9.

10.

USE THE VALUE YOU PROVIDE TO CUSTOMERS AS A MAJOR BOOST TO EMPLOYEE MORALE, PRIDE, AND TEAMWORK

What are seven steps you could take that would increase the value that customers get from your products or services?

1.

2.

3.

4.

5.

6.

7.

STUDY WAYS TO "MAXIMIZE VALUE INCREMENTALLY"

PILLAR 3

REFINE TO PERFECT PRICING

PILLAR 3: REFINE TO PERFECT PRICING

How you price your products or services has a significant impact on business success from several perspectives. It impacts the way customers view your company and also significantly drives the financial performance of the company as a whole. Pricing is a complex activity and should be looked at from several perspectives (cost driven, competitive analysis, image impact, and others) as a starting point, but should also be revised and updated based on market feedback. Developing the right pricing approach is an ongoing activity in successful companies.

The pillar suggests refining to perfect pricing. What would perfect pricing look like in your business? What would cause your pricing to be less than perfect? What are five changes you could make to bring your pricing closer to perfect? (pp 65 – 66)

1.

2.

3.

4.

5.

UNDERSTAND WHAT PERFECT PRICING LOOKS LIKE IN YOUR BUSINESS

On a scale of 1 to 10 (with 10 being perfect), how well do you understand the true / entire costs of the products or services you sell? How could you improve your cost accounting to have better information to assist with pricing decisions? (pp 67 – 70)

UNDERSTAND THE TRUE COSTS OF THE PRODUCTS AND SERVICES YOU SELL

THE BOOK DISCUSSES SIX METHODS OF PRICING, WHICH ARE LISTED BELOW:

1. Margin Based
2. Income Based
3. Competitive Based
4. Volume Based
5. Image Based
6. Testing Based

In reviewing the six different methods, which ones have you used in determining your existing approach? Which ones have you ignored? How will you change your pricing approach after seeing these different methods? (pp 66)

USE SIX DIFFERENT APPROACHES TO DETERMINING YOUR PRICING

How do you use the concept of "managing margins" to run your business? (pp 67 – 70)

Compare your current margin rates to the industry. How are you doing? Why? What needs to be done? (pp 67 – 70)

The book provides a list of margin tendencies – based on your understanding of your products what are some of the margin tendencies that may impact the pricing approach of your company?

Margins Tend to Be Higher	Margins Tend to Be Lower
Proprietary / unique items	Commodities / undifferentiated products
Early in product life cycle	Later in product life cycle
Lower volume items	Higher volume items
Slower moving inventory	Faster moving inventory
Higher risk customers	Lower risk customers

MANAGING MARGINS IS A SIGNIFICANT MANAGEMENT ELEMENT IN MOST BUSINESSES

How does your pricing structure impact your personal income goals? (pp 71 – 72)

What impact would a 10% increase in your pricing (assuming the same volume) have on the overall profitability of the business (or your personal income if you own the business)? (pp 71 – 72)

PRICING HAS A SIGNIFICANT IMPACT ON THE PROFITABILITY OF A BUSINESS AND THE INCOME OF THOSE IN IT

What is the range of pricing within your industry? Where do you plan to fit into that range? Why? (pp 71 – 73)

What steps have you taken to analyze the competition's approach to pricing? How could you improve this approach? (pp 71 – 73)

Here is a form to assist with a competitive pricing analysis: (pp 71 – 73)

Competitor	Similar Product or Service	Cost	Comments

STUDY THE COMPETITION TO UNDERSTAND THEIR PRICING APPROACH

What does your current pricing approach say about your company? What image does your pricing portray about your company? (pp 73 – 74)

Looking at other companies in your industry, how have they used pricing to create a certain image? Have they been effective? Are there any valuable lessons for you there? (pp 73 – 74)

How could you use pricing to improve the image you desire in the marketplace? (pp 73 – 74)

PRICING IMPACTS YOUR COMPANY IMAGE – USE IT TO YOUR ADVANTAGE

What impact do changes in pricing have on your volume? Why is the pricing level you have chosen the right one in relation to pricing, margins, and volume? Does this approach maximize your extended margins? (pp 74 – 76)

Construct a Price / Volume / Margin Analysis for your business: (pp 74 – 76)

Price						
Cost						
Volume						
Margin Per Unit						
GM %						
Extended Sales						
Extended GM $						

PRICING IMPACTS THE EXPECTED VOLUME OF YOUR PRODUCTS – SEEK THE LEVEL THAT GENERATES THE LARGEST OVERALL, EXTENDED MARGIN

Finding "perfect" pricing is never easy to do. List ten ways you could test your pricing or learn from the market which pricing approach will be the most profitable to your company. (pp 76 – 77)

1.

2.

3.

4.

5.

6.

7.

8.

9.

10.

USE TESTING TO REFINE TO PERFECT PRICING

How do you approach the situation when you are not the lowest priced company in the market? How have you trained your employees to handle this situation? (pp 78 – 79)

What are five things you tell customers when they observe that you are not the lowest priced company in the industry. How confident do you feel about these answers? (pp 78 – 79)

1.

2.

3.

4.

5.

BE ABLE TO CONFIDENTLY EXPLAIN WHY YOU ARE NOT THE LOWEST COST PROVIDER IN THE INDUSTRY

Do you ever provide products or services for FREE? List seven ways you could use a free strategy to your advantage? (pp 79 – 81)

1.

2.

3.

4.

5.

6.

7.

How do those "free" strategies lead to significantly larger revenues in the future? (pp 79 – 81)

OFTEN FREE STRATEGIES CAN BE VERY POWERFUL FOR MARKETING EFFORTS

Very often a "free with purchase" strategy works extremely well. List five ways you could do this. (pp 79 – 81)

1.

2.

3.

4.

5.

Describe how these approaches will increase your sales. (pp 79 – 81)

FREE WITH PURCHASE CAN BE A SIGNIFICANT MARKETING STRATEGY

What impact does discounting have on your company? How do you calculate the margin impact of discounting within your company? How much must your volumes increase to compensate for any discounting you are doing? (pp 82 – 83)

	Before Discount	After Discount
Sell Price		
Cost		
$ Margin Per Item		A.
Gross Margin %		
Margin at 100 Units	B.	
Units Required to Generate Same Margin	100	C.
Required Increase in Volume	0%	D.

$C = B \div A$
$D = (C\text{-}100) \div 100$

DISCOUNTS CAN HAVE A SURPRISINGLY SIGNIFICANT IMPACT ON MARGINS – FULLY UNDERSTAND HOW THIS ANALYISIS IMPACTS YOUR BUSINESS

Are there ways to use payment terms to your advantage in your business? Are there ways for them to improve your profitability? (pp 84)

What are the ramifications of doing this?

TERMS CAN PRESENT PROFIT OPPORTUNITIES

How does your pricing reflect your personal confidence in your business? If you were significantly more confident, would you change your pricing? How? (pp 88)

YOUR CONFIDENCE IS OFTEN REFLECTED IN YOUR PRICING

List ten changes you would make to make your pricing more perfect.

1.

2.

3.

4.

5.

6.

7.

8.

9.

10.

REFINE TO PERFECT PRICING

FORM PRODUCTIVE LINKING RELATIONSHIPS

PILLAR 4: FORM PRODUCTIVE LINKING RELATIONSHIPS

In many businesses, there are significant people and organizations that "link" customers to your company. This can be as informal as a casual referral from an existing customer to as complex as a multifaceted approach to distribution. Generating positive word of mouth advertising should be the goal of any company, but should not be just left to chance. The company should take proactive steps to ensure these various types of linking relationships are constructed to facilitate significant forward momentum for business. Who is important to link you to your end customers?

List ten people or companies who have been important to linking your company to customers in the past. How have they impacted your sales? Which had the greatest positive impact on revenues? (pp 92)

1.

2.

3.

4.

5.

6.

7.

8.

9.

10.

LINKING RELATIONSHIPS SERVE AN IMPORTANT ROLE IN BUILDING A COMPANY

Imagine your only revenue strategy was to have ten very influential individuals tell others about your company. Who would those people be? Why? How would they help you develop your business? (pp 92 – 95)

1.

2.

3.

4.

5.

6.

7.

8.

9.

10.

Who would be on this list if you could expand it to 100?

CONSIDER WHO YOUR MOST IMPORTANT LINKERS ARE

Describe how the following linking relationships could positively impact your company. (pp 92)

Referral Partners

Distribution Partners

Strategic Alliances

Key Influencers

CONSIDER THE DIFFERENT TYPES OF LINKING RELATIONSHIPS

How do your linkers benefit from connecting you to customers? What are five things of value you create for them? (pp 96 – 97)

1.

2.

3.

4.

5.

TAKE A PARTNERSHIP APPROACH TO LINKERS

List ten ways you could better incorporate reinforcements and rewards when people assist you in growing your company. (pp 96-97)

1.

2.

3.

4.

5.

6.

7.

8.

9.

10.

LOOK FOR WAYS TO REINFORCE AND REWARD LINKERS

Have you ever considered compensating people (or companies) for their referrals? How would that work in your company? (pp 96 – 97)

CONSIDER MULTIPLE WAYS TO POSITIVELY REINFORCE LINKING BEHAVIOR, EVEN COMPENSATION

Word of mouth advertising is one of the most common ways that people seek to build their businesses. What are seven ways you could become more proactive about generating referrals instead of just letting them happen? (pp 97 – 99)

1.

2.

3.

4.

5.

6.

7.

BE PROACTIVE ABOUT FEEDING WORD OF MOUTH ADVERTISING – IT CAN HAPPEN ON ITS OWN WITHOUT YOUR PROMPTING, BUT IT WILL DO SO ON ITS OWN TIME FRAME

In what ways does networking impact the development of your customer revenue streams? What are three networking opportunities you could invest time into which would result in a significant increase in the number of referrals coming your way?

1.

2.

3.

USE NETWORKING TO INCREASE YOUR LINKING RELATIONSHIPS

What are five steps you could take to make it REALLY EASY for people to make referrals to your business? (Assume it is very difficult for people to refer to you now, what could you do to make it much simpler?) (pp 99 – 100)

1.

2.

3.

4.

5.

MAKE IT EASY FOR LINKERS TO CONNECT OTHERS TO YOU

List seven ways that you could develop ongoing and regular communications with referral partners. How could you remind them to send you referrals? How do you stay "top of mind" with them? (pp 99 – 100)

1.

2.

3.

4.

5.

6.

7.

KEEP IN TOUCH WITH REFERRAL PARTNERS – REMIND THEM WHY THEY SHOULD CONTINUE TO SEND CUSTOMERS YOUR WAY

Describe how your company uses or could use distribution partners to link to end customers? (pp 102 – 105)

CONSIDER DISTRIBUTION OPPORTUNITIES IN YOUR BUSINESS

What are five specific goals you hope to accomplish with distribution partners? How well are you doing? How do you do better? (pp 102 – 105)

1.

2.

3.

4.

5.

HAVE SPECIFIC GOALS FOR YOUR DISTRIBUTION PROGRAM

Assume that tomorrow your current method of distribution becomes obsolete overnight, and you need to develop alternate methods of bringing your products or services to customers. What are six alternate approaches you could take? (pp 106 – 109)

1.

2.

3.

4.

5.

6.

CONSIDER DISTRIBUTION ALTERNATIVES

What are five things you can do to better communicate with your distribution partners? (pp 106 – 109)

1.

2.

3.

4.

5.

COMMUNICATION IS VITAL TO SUCCEED WITH DISTRIBUTION

Describe in detail how you approach distribution from a partnership perspective. How do you positively impact their company(ies)? (pp 106 – 107)

CREATE ATTRACTIVE, PROFITABLE BUSINESS OPPORTUNITIES FOR DISTRIBUTION PARTNERS – BE AN IMPORTANT PART OF THEIR BUSINESS

For each level in the distribution system, list the pricing / discount structure and describe how each level can be profitable with that arrangement. (pp 105 – 107)

ENSURE YOUR PRICING AND DISCOUNTING APPROACH PROVIDES SUFFICIENT PROFIT OPPORTUNITIES TO EVERYONE IN THE DISTRIBUTION CHANNEL

List three additional ways to facilitate movement of products and services through the entire distribution system. How do you ensure success for everyone? (pp 108 – 109)

1.

2.

3.

FOCUS ON MOVING PRODUCTS AND SERVICES THROUGHOUT THE ENTIRE DISTRIBUTION CHANNEL

In what ways does channel conflict impact your distribution approaches? How do you manage/minimize this? (pp 107)

STUDY WAYS TO REDUCE CHANNEL CONFLICT IN DISTRIBUTION SYSTEMS

List seven ways you could better collect "best practices" from your successful distribution partners and share them with others. (pp 108)

1.

2.

3.

4.

5.

6.

7.

STUDY BEST PRACTICES FROM YOUR DISTRIBUTION PARTNERS AND SHARE THEM TO HELP OTHERS IMPROVE

How do you ensure you do not become overly-reliant on any single distribution partner? Do you have backups in place in key areas? How vulnerable are you regarding a concentration of key distribution partners? (pp 108 – 109)

LOOK FOR WAYS TO HAVE BACKUPS AND ALTERNATIVES TO DISTRIBUTION PARTNERS TO PREVENT BEING TOO RELIANT ON THEM WITHIN YOUR BUSINESS

If you are in the middle of the distribution system, in what ways can you be more demanding of your suppliers? (pp 110 – 113)

BE DEMANDING OF SUPPLIERS

How could "wide" distribution growth strategies promote your company's development? How can you greatly expand your business while maintaining your same role in a distribution system? (pp 113)

How might "deep" distribution approaches facilitate the growth of your business? How could you significantly increase your business by expanding the role you play in the distribution system? (pp 113)

CONSIDER BOTH WIDE AND DEEP STRATEGIES FOR EXPANSION IF YOU ARE IN THE MIDDLE OF A DISTRIBUTION SYSTEM

What are five ways your suppliers have assisted you in improving your approach to customers? Have you asked them about best practices with others they sell to? How might you collect more information from them? (pp 112)

1.

2.

3.

4.

5.

USE SUPPLIERS AS SOURCES OF INFORMATION TO HELP YOU BUILD CUSTOMER REVENUES

How have you built supplier options into your business? Are you single sourced in any situations? What impact does this have on the security of your growth? (pp 112)

HAVE BACKUP VENDORS AND OTHER OPTIONS

List five important strategic partnerships you could enter into with other companies that would greatly improve your marketing approach? (pp 114 – 118)

1.

2.

3.

4.

5.

USE STRATEGIC MARKETING ALLIANCES AS A GROWTH STRATEGY

Can you private label (or OEM) your products or services? How might this create a significant growth opportunity? List several approaches. (pp 114 – 118)

CONSIDER WAYS TO PRIVATE LABEL YOUR PRODUCTS OR SERVICES FOR OTHERS

Consider your customer development approaches. How might other companies want to leverage into those competencies through marketing partnerships? (pp 114 – 118)

What weaknesses do you have in approaching the market? Are there other companies that you could partner with to shore up those weaknesses? (pp 114 – 118)

CONSIDER YOUR STRENGTHS AND WEAKNESSES TO UNCOVER STRATEGIC PARNTERSHIP OPPORTUNITIES

How might you partner with your COMPETITORS to mutually build your business? (pp 117)

LOOK FOR WAYS TO WORK WITH YOUR COMPETITORS

List twenty businesses who serve the same target market as yours, but are not direct competitors? How could you work with these companies? (pp 116 -118)

1.

2.

3.

4.

5.

6.

7.

8.

9.

10.

11.

12.

13.

14.

15.

16.

17.

18.

19.

20.

CONSIDER OTHER COMPANIES YOU COULD WORK WITH TO DEVELOP UNIQUE, MUTUALLY BENEFICIAL APPROACHES TO THE MARKET

Who significantly influences your target market? How do they impact the customer's purchase decisions? How can you get them to positively influence your customers? How can they help (or hurt) your customer efforts? (pp 118 – 120)

STUDY THE KEY INFLUENCERS WHO WILL IMPACT HOW YOUR CUSTOMERS VIEW YOUR EFFORTS

List ten ways you could "form productive linking relationships" and significantly expand your company.

1.

2.

3.

4.

5.

6.

7.

8.

9.

10.

USE LINKING RELATIONSHIPS AS A POWERFUL WAY TO GROW

PILLAR 5

SHARPEN YOUR COMPETITIVE EDGE

PILLAR 5: SHARPEN YOUR COMPETITIVE EDGE

Is your industry more or less competitive than it was five years ago? In most instances, a company operates in a very competitive environment. This is particularly true when you expand the notion of competitors to also include indirect and "do nothing" competitive elements. Helping your customer answer the question "Why should I choose you over the other options?" is an important part of growing a business. Having a competitive edge is not an "all or nothing" thing and you should focus on ways to continually improve its strength.

List ten reasons that customers should choose your business over other options:
(pp 123 – 124)

1.

2.

3.

4.

5.

6.

7.

8.

9.

10.

STUDY WHY CUSTOMERS SHOULD CHOOSE YOUR BUSINESS

There are 3 kinds of competitors of competitive forces:

Direct Competitors – sell essentially the same kind of product to similar customers
Indirect Competitors – cater to same customers, but in a different, less direct way
Do Nothing Competitors – when the customer does not take any action

Example: If you are a bowling alley, the other bowling alley in your town is a direct competitor, the movie theatre is an indirect competitor (as you are both competing for the customer's entertainment dollars), and staying at home watching TV is a "do nothing" competitor.

List your top five, most significant competitors in each category. (pp 125 – 126)

Direct Competitors	Indirect Competitors	Do Nothing Competitors

IDENTIFY THE TOP DIRECT, INDIRECT, AND DO NOTHING COMPETITORS

When looking at the three types of competitors (direct, indirect, and do nothing), how do each impact your business differently? Which one is the most threatening to your business? Which ones create the most opportunities for expansion? (pp 125 – 126)

STUDY HOW THE DIFFERENT TYPES OF COMPETITORS IMPACT YOUR BUSINESS AND HOW THEY CREATE OPPORTUNITIES

In looking at your competitors, what do they do well? What are their strengths? How does this impact your business? (pp 127 – 132)

Competitor	Strength	Impact on Your Biz

LOOK CLOSELY AT THE STRENGTHS OF YOUR COMPETITORS

What do they do poorly? What are their weaknesses? How does this impact your business? (pp 127 – 132)

Competitor	Weakness	Impact on Your Biz

LOOK CLOSELY AT THE WEAKNESSES OF YOUR COMPETITORS

When looking at competitors, it is important to consider them from the perspective of the market, not necessarily our own. For your most significant competitors, describe how they position themselves in the market and also how you believe the market perceives them. (pp 127 – 132)

Competitor	How They Position Themselves in the Market	How the Market Perceives Them

STUDY HOW THE MARKET PERCEIVES YOUR COMPETITORS

We tend to focus on the negatives of our competitors and why we are superior to them. However, if your competitors have customers, then someone is picking them over you. List ten reasons you believe customers may be picking their businesses over yours. (pp 127 – 132)

1.

2.

3.

4.

5.

6.

7.

8.

9.

10.

STUDY WHY CUSTOMERS SELECT YOUR COMPETITORS OVER YOU

Often competitors are doing things well that we can take advantage of and build upon. List seven things they are doing that you could tap into. For each list what you have to do to take advantage of this. (pp 127 – 132)

Competitor	What Are They Doing Well That You Can Leverage Upon?	What Do You Need to Do to Take Advantage of This?

FIND WAYS TO TAKE ADVANTAGE OF THE THINGS YOUR COMPETITORS ARE DOING WELL

Our tendency is to get fairly biased when we study the competition. Describe how this might impact your evaluation of the competition and how can you de-emotionalize this process. (pp 127 – 132)

DE-EMOTIONALIZE THE PROCESS OF STUDYING THE COMPETITION — YOU GET LESS VALUE FROM THIS EFFORT IF YOU ARE COMING FROM A VERY BIASED PERSPECTIVE

Conduct a SWOT Analysis to describe your position in relation to all of the competitors in your industry. (pp 127 – 132)

STRENGTHS	WEAKNESSES
OPPORTUNITIES	THREATS

Conduct a SWOT Analysis to compare your business to one of your major competitors.

COMPETITOR = _____

STRENGTHS	WEAKNESSES
OPPORTUNITIES	THREATS

Conduct a SWOT Analysis to compare your business to one of your major competitors.

COMPETITOR = _____

STRENGTHS	WEAKNESSES
OPPORTUNITIES	THREATS

Conduct a SWOT Analysis to compare your business to one of your major competitors.

COMPETITOR = _____

STRENGTHS	WEAKNESSES
OPPORTUNITIES	THREATS

Conduct a SWOT Analysis to compare your business to one of your major competitors.

COMPETITOR = _____

STRENGTHS	WEAKNESSES
OPPORTUNITIES	THREATS

Conduct a SWOT Analysis to compare your business to one of your major competitors.

COMPETITOR = _____

STRENGTHS	WEAKNESSES
OPPORTUNITIES	THREATS

When you study your competitors, what are five key gaps in the market you fill that are not addressed by others? How do you address these voids? (pp 127 – 132)

1.

2.

3.

4.

5.

DESIGN YOUR COMPETITIVE EDGE TO FILL KEY GAPS IN THE MARKET

List five key approaches you take in selling against the competition? (pp 127 – 132)

1.

2.

3.

4.

5.

SPECIFY HOW YOU WILL SELL AGAINST THE COMPETITION

List seven interesting things competitors might say to prospective customers when they sell against you? What insights can you gain from this? (pp 127 – 132)

1.

2.

3.

4.

5.

6.

7.

STUDY WHAT THE COMPETITION WILL SAY WHEN THEY SELL AGAINST YOU

Of your competitors, who are the three you feel least comfortable selling against? WHY? (pp 127 – 132)

1.

2.

3.

STUDY THE COMPETITORS YOU LEAST LIKE TO SELL AGAINST

Explain your competitive edge in less than two sentences. How can you shorten your USP (Unique Selling Position) to make it more succinct and powerful? (pp 132 – 136)

SUCCINCTLY EXPLAIN YOUR COMPETITVE EDGE

COMPETITIVE EDGE FORM

OUR COMPETITIVE EDGE .... (RATE EACH POINT ON SCALE OF 1 TO 10.)

is meaningful to the customer

| 1 | 2 | 3 | 4 | 5 | 6 | 7 | 8 | 9 | 10 |

fills important unmet needs

| 1 | 2 | 3 | 4 | 5 | 6 | 7 | 8 | 9 | 10 |

motivates the customer to action

| 1 | 2 | 3 | 4 | 5 | 6 | 7 | 8 | 9 | 10 |

is unique and difficult to duplicate

| 1 | 2 | 3 | 4 | 5 | 6 | 7 | 8 | 9 | 10 |

can be communicated effectively

| 1 | 2 | 3 | 4 | 5 | 6 | 7 | 8 | 9 | 10 |

can be sustained

| 1 | 2 | 3 | 4 | 5 | 6 | 7 | 8 | 9 | 10 |

is well-defined

| 1 | 2 | 3 | 4 | 5 | 6 | 7 | 8 | 9 | 10 |

can be quantified

| 1 | 2 | 3 | 4 | 5 | 6 | 7 | 8 | 9 | 10 |

is consistent

| 1 | 2 | 3 | 4 | 5 | 6 | 7 | 8 | 9 | 10 |

is very marketable

| 1 | 2 | 3 | 4 | 5 | 6 | 7 | 8 | 9 | 10 |

TOTAL SCORE (OUT OF 100) _____

SCORE YOUR COMPETITIVE EDGE

Of the ten characteristics of a strong competitive edge, which are your strengths? Weaknesses? How can you improve? How can you make improvements in this area an ongoing and continuous process? (pp 132 – 136)

Strengths:

Weaknesses:

Opportunities to improve:

CONSIDER THE TEN WAYS TO GRADE YOUR COMPETITIVE EDGE

How is your competitive edge meaningful to the customer? List five ways to make it MORE meaningful to them. (pp 133)

1.

2.

3.

4.

5.

SEEK WAYS TO MAKE YOUR COMPETITIVE EDGE MORE MEANINFUL TO CUSTOMERS

How does your competitive edge address unmet customer needs? List three ways you could design your edge to better meet these unmet needs? (pp 133)

1.

2.

3.

YOUR EDGE SHOULD ADDRESS UNMET CUSTOMER NEEDS

What are four things you could do to make your competitive edge more difficult to copy? (pp 133 – 134)

1.

2.

3.

4.

SEEK WAYS TO MAKE YOUR EDGE MORE DIFFICULT TO COPY

How easy is it to understand your competitive edge? Describe five ways you could make it more simple and straightforward? (pp 134)

1.

2.

3.

4.

5.

YOUR COMPETITIVE EDGE SHOULD BE EASY TO UNDERSTAND

Is your competitive edge sustainable? What must you do inside your company to ensure you can continue to deliver your edge with consistency? (pp 134)

DEVELOP AN EDGE WHICH CAN STAND THE TEST OF TIME

How would you rate the focus of your edge? How can you make it more defined and precise? (pp 134)

YOUR EDGE SHOULD BE VERY FOCUSED AND PRECISE

How can you quantify your edge? Specifically, how much better are you than others in the marketplace? (pp 135)

QUANTIFY YOUR EDGE

How could you improve the marketability of your competitive edge? Describe how your edge is one you could build a business upon. (pp 135)

BE ABLE TO BASE A MARKETING EFFORT ON YOUR COMPETITIVE EDGE

What are three messages you need to share with customers based around your competitive edge? (pp 123 - 139)

1.

2.

3.

TRANSLATE YOUR COMPETITIVE EDGE INTO KEY MESSAGES

Your competitive edge can be used within the company as an outstanding team building process, including non-marketing and non-management employees. List ten ways you could use your competitive edge to build teamwork and morale. (pp 136 – 137)

1.

2.

3.

4.

5.

6.

7.

8.

9.

10.

USE YOUR COMPETITIVE EDGE TO BUILD YOUR TEAM

PILLAR 6

CONNECT POWERFULLY WITH CUSTOMERS

PILLAR 6: CONNECT POWERFULLY WITH CUSTOMERS

What if customers do not know about you or do not fully understand all the wonderful things you have to offer them? That's not a theoretical situation, its reality! What you do to communicate and make lasting relationships with customers will significantly impact your revenue levels. Customer communications is a broad area which includes selling, branding, advertising, public relations, and numerous other ways your company communicates with customers. Being conscious about the messages you share, how you deliver them, and how to measure your success is vitally important. No one buys from you if they don't know you exist!

You look at your product or service very differently than your customers do. (If they saw your company the same way you did, they all would buy. Wouldn't they!?!) What are the five key gaps between how the customer views your company, product, or service and how you would like them to view them? What are five ways you use communication techniques to bridge these gaps with the customer? (pp 140 – 142)

Communication Gaps	Ways to Fill Them

LOOK FOR AND FILL KEY COMMUNICATION GAPS

What are three ways your customers misunderstand your company? How do you correct this? (pp 140 – 142)

1.

2.

3.

CLEAR UP MISUNDERSTANDINGS CUSTOMERS MAY HAVE ABOUT YOUR COMPANY

If you could transplant five key ideas directly from your head into the minds of your customers or prospective customers, what would they be? (pp 140 – 142)

1.

2.

3.

4.

5.

IDENTIFY KEY IDEAS YOU WISH TO PLANT IN THE MINDS OF CUSTOMERS

What is the ideal way you would like your customers to view your product or service? What do you have to accomplish for them to view it that way? Be specific. (pp 140 – 142)

UNDERSTAND THE WAY YOU WANT CUSTOMERS TO VIEW YOUR COMPANY

OBJECTIVES OF CUSTOMER COMMUNICATIONS

- Communicate the benefits the customer will derive from using your product or service

- Create curiosity so the customer is interested in learning more

- Resonate / connect with the market in a way that they are drawn to develop a relationship with your company

- Construct the firm's image, reputation, and goodwill (the warm and fuzzies)

- Generate familiarity and trust

- Educate and persuade

- Communicate the advantage of your company over other options

- Clarify the purchase decisions or steps the customer should consider in evaluating a purchase

- Show the customer the next step

- Manage expectations, both building them up, but also keeping them realistic such that the company can deliver upon promises

- Reinforce the purchase decision after the transaction

What are the five most important objectives of your customer communications program? Specifically, what are you trying to accomplish by communicating with customers? Be detailed. (pp 142 – 144)

1.

2.

3.

4.

5.

DEVELOP COMMUNICATION APPROACHES WITH KEY OBJECTIVES IN MIND

A benefit is what the customer gets out of the products or services you sell (versus a feature, which describes the product or service.) What are the seven most significant benefits your customers will derive from your product or service? How do you put that, succinctly, into words? (pp 143)

1.

2.

3.

4.

5.

6.

7.

EXPLAIN TO CUSTOMERS THE BENEFITS OF DOING BUSINESS WITH YOU

What are three things you could incorporate into your communications messages that would make the customer curious and would make them want to learn more? What are some "teaser" statements or questions you could use that would peak the interest of customers? (pp 143)

1.

2.

3.

CREATE CURIOSITY WITH CUSTOMERS

What are seven things you could say to your customers that would deepen the relationship they have with you? (pp 143)

1.

2.

3.

4.

5.

6.

7.

INTENSIFY YOUR RELATIONSHIP WITH CUSTOMERS

How deeply do customers trust you? What could you communicate that would build a greater level of connection between you and customers? (pp 143)

BUILD THE TRUST OF YOUR CUSTOMER BASE

What are ten things you could educate your customer about? (pp 143)

1.

2.

3.

4.

5.

6.

7.

8.

9.

10.

EDUCATE CUSTOMERS WITH YOUR MARKETING MESSAGES

Incorporating your competitive edge into your marketing messages is an important step. How is your edge used in your customer communications approach? Do your marketing messages reinforce your competitive edge? (pp 143)

CONVEY YOUR COMPETITIVE EDGE IN YOUR MESSAGES

When you communicate with customers, what is the next step you want them to take? How do you specify this? How can you be more specific in directing customers on the actions you would like them to take? (Don't assume customers will figure out what they should do next!) (pp 143)

SPECIFY THE NEXT STEP

How does the M-Cubed Method of Customer Communications (Message, Method/ Media, and Measurement) impact the growth and development of your company? If you look at each step, where are there opportunities to improve? (pp 144 – 145)

Message	Method / Media	Measurement

USE THE M-CUBED METHOD TO ORGANIZE CUSTOMER COMMUNICATIONS

Study the following list of common types of customer messages, which ones do you currently utilize in your marketing messages? Which ones would you like to include in the future? (pp 145 – 147)

COMMON TYPES OF CUSTOMER MESSAGES

- We solve a problem – this problem bothers you
- We are better than the competition – you will be better off with us
- We are a better value – don't waste your money elsewhere
- We are lower priced – you spend less here
- We are discounting – you get our best prices
- We have developed something new – you need something new
- We have made an improvement – your life will be better
- We are trustworthy – you can be confident in us
- We have a time-based special – you don't want to miss out
- We appreciate you / thank you – you will feel appreciated
- We want your referrals – you want to tell people about good things
- We make your life easier – you want an easier life
- We make you more money – you want more money
- We make you more popular / admired – you want to be more popular
- We make you like yourself more – you want to like yourself
- We help you avoid pain – you have pain you want to get rid of
- We help reduce your stress – you have a rough life and deserve better
- We are making it easy to trial our product – you have nothing to lose
- We offer great guarantees / warranties – you won't be disappointed
- We are your friends – you want to associate with us
- We are interested in the same things you are – you really like us
- We want to build a relationship with you – you want to know us
- We are fun, unique, and interesting – you will enjoy our interactions
- We give you peace of mind – you crave this

STUDY COMMON MESSAGES FOR ASSISTANCE IN DEVELOPING YOURS

Complete the following message development exercise: Imagine that you are given 30 minutes with your most valuable prospective customer. In detail, what would you tell them? What are the key messages you wish to share with customers? List them, organize them, then rank them in order of importance. (pp 147 – 148)

REFINE YOUR MESSAGES WITH THE "30 MINUTE" EXERCISE

As you look at the various messages you wish to share with customers, do you see some logical organization and key groupings? Does this help you refine your messages? (pp 147 – 148)

GROUP YOUR MESSAGES INTO A LOGICAL ORDER

Use the following 22 point message development checklist to develop better messages. (pp 148 – 156)

___ Your messages do not beat around the bush – they establish relevance quickly
___ You use headlines and subheads to keep the prospect interested
___ You focus on benefits over features
___ You have included your competitive edge
___ Your messages are focused and narrow
___ You summarize with bullet points and numbered lists
___ Your messages use branding and interesting names
___ You focus on defining the problem and providing a solution
___ Your messages relate with their frustrations
___ You verbalize what you want *for* the customer and what you want *from* them
___ Your messages appeal to the emotions of customers and touch their hot buttons
___ You paint mind pictures so the customer can visualize solutions
___ You make the communications "risk free" for the customer
___ Your messages create urgency and create a fear of loss
___ You use powerful words that most connect with customers (see list below)
___ Your messages avoid trite overused clichés
___ You address common objections (see list below) in your messages
___ You provide clear and precise instructions on what the customer is to do next
___ Your messages do not over-promise
___ Your messages clarify what your product / service / company is not
___ Your messages share testimonials
___ Your messages have a personality

What methods do you employ to quickly capture the attention of your customers? What could you do to establish relevance with customers more quickly in the ways you interact with them? (pp 150)

ESTABLISH RELEVANCE QUICKLY

FEATURES describe your product, service, or company. BENEFITS, however, describe the positive results the customer gets from them. Explain the difference between features and benefits in your business? How do you use this to communicate with customers? (pp 150)

USE BENEFITS BEFORE FEATURES

Show an example of how you could simplify your messages using bullet points and numbered lists. (pp 151)

USE BULLET POINTS AND NUMBERED LISTS

How do you use branding to create a common thread throughout your customer messages? What is the brand you use? List seven ways it runs through your messages as a common theme. (pp 151)

1.

2.

3.

4.

5.

6.

7.

USE BRANDING TO TIE YOUR MESSAGES TOGETHER

Great messages define a problem, then present a solution. (Point out the itch, then scratch it! How could you incorporate this with your company? (pp 151)

DEFINE THE PROBLEM, AGITATE IT, THEN SOLVE IT

How can you interweave a discussion about the frustrations your customers deal with? How can you communicate that your company can help ease those frustrations? (pp 151)

HIGHLIGHT KEY CUSTOMER FRUSTRATIONS

Improve your messages by describing what you want for your customers. Pointing out "what's in it for me" can greatly help your marketing communications. List five ways that you can describe the things you want for your customers. (pp 152)

1.

2.

3.

4.

5.

TELL THE CUSTOMER THE GOOD THINGS YOU WANT FOR THEM

How do your messages make an emotional appeal to your customers? Do you touch their hot buttons? How could you improve? List five of the emotional hot buttons you push. (pp 152)

1.

2.

3.

4.

5.

APPEAL TO KEY EMOTIONAL HOT BUTTONS

Study the list of power words below. Highlight or circle the ones you believe could apply to your customer communication messages. How can you use these words to strengthen your messages. (pp 153)

Words that connect with customers (the top 25)

announcing, benefit / benefits, better, comprehensive, custom, easy / easier, free / free trial, introducing, limited time, professional, proven, quality, quickly, risk-free, sample, satisfaction, save / savings , serve / service, simple / simplified, superior, tested, ultimate, value, win / winning, you / your

Words that connect with customers (225 more)

absolute / absolutely, advantage, advice, affordable, aggressive / aggressively, amazing, ambitious, astonishing, at last, attractive, authentic, awesome, bargain, beautiful, breakthrough, can I ask a favor, capable, care about, cash, challenge / challenging, chock full, choice, client, colorful, colossal, compare, competitive, complete, concern / concerned , confidential, conservative, convenience, count on us, cram-packed, customer, definite, delight / delighted / delightful, delivered, desire, desperate, determined, direct, discount, discover, driving, ecstatic, effective / effectively, efficient / efficiency, emerging, endorsed / endorsement, energy, enhanced, enormous, enthusiastically, envision, established, excellence / excellent, exciting, exclusive, experience / experienced, expert / expertise, extensive, fact, fantastic, fascinating, fast, first, focus, formula, fortunate, fortune, frustrated / frustration, genuine, gigantic, good, great / greatest, grow / growth, guarantee, health, help / helpful, high tech, highest, highly desirable, honest / honestly, how to, huge, hurry, if, then, imagine, immediately, important, improved, income stream, incredible / incredibly, inexpensive, informative / information, ingenious, innovative / innovation, insider, inspiring, instructions, integrity, intelligent, interesting, just arrived, just in time, key, knowledgeable, largest, last chance, last minute, lasting, latest, launching, lavish, liberal, lifetime, love, lowest, luxurious, magic, maximum, miracle, money, monumental, more than, never sacrifice, new, newly released, no compromise, no questions asked, notable, noted, now, opportunities, outstanding, partnership, passionate, patented, paying too much, personalized, pertinent, phenomenal, pioneer, popular, positively, potential, powerful, practical, prestigious, proficiency, profitability, profits, prominent, promise, promising, proprietary, reasonable, reduced, refund, reliable, remarkable, renowned, reputation, return on investment, revealing, revolutionary, reward, sale, salient, secrets, select, sensational, serious / seriously, shocking truth, significant, sizable, skill, solution, special, specialize, spectacular, start now, strategic / strategies, stress / stressful, strong, substantial, successful, super, sure fire, surprise, take control, terrific, testimony / testimonial, thorough, time sensitive, timely, tired of, today, track record, tremendous, trial, truth, unconditional, unique, unlimited, unlock, unparalleled, unsurpassed, unusual, urgent, useful, valuable, visualize, vitality, want / wanted, want good things, warranty, wealth, window of opportunity, wonderful, world famous, worry / worried, yes

USE POWER WORDS

Often your messages make perfect sense to you, but customers have a more difficult time envisioning the benefits you are proposing. How could you paint mind pictures which help your customers better visualize the benefits they could derive from your company? (pp 152)

PAINT MIND PICTURES

Many times customers are interested in what we are selling, but not motivated to take immediate action. Very often, this means we need to increase the urgency with which we ask customers to act. What are three ways you could increase the urgency of the customers and create (or reinforce) a fear of loss? (pp 153)

1.

2.

3.

CREATE URGENCY

What are the common objections that will surface when you present your marketing messages to your customers? Use this list of common objections to help identify objections to your communications. How can you address these common objections in advance in your communications? (pp 154)

COMMON OBJECTIONS

- I don't have enough time
- I cannot afford it
- The purchase is not necessary
- I would like to purchase, but must wait
- Your solution may work for others, but it will not work for me

- I have already solved that problem
- I already buy from your competition
- I am skeptical and not sure I believe you
- I don't believe your solution will work
- I am not the decision maker
- I need to check with my boss

Anticipated Objections	How You Will Answer Them in Advance

ANTICIPATE OBJECTIONS AND ANSWER THEM IN ADVANCE

How can you incorporate testimonials in your messages to bring third party credibility to your messages? (pp 156)

USE THIRD PARTY TESTIMONIALS TO INCREASE YOUR CREDIBILITY

Often marketing messages are unoriginal, trite, and boring. How can you increase the personality of your marketing messages? Are you too boring? List seven ways you could spice it up. (pp 156)

1.

2.

3.

4.

5.

6.

7.

SPICE UP YOUR MESSAGES WITH SOME PERSONALITY

Circle the different ways you currently communicate with customers (deliver messages). Mark those you pay for with a "P" and those that are free (or nearly free) with an "F". If there are other methods of communication you use, list them below. (pp 157 – 161)

METHODS FOR MESSAGE DELIVERY / MEDIA OPTIONS

- Daily Communications – Invoices, shipping boxes, presentation folders, answering the phone
- Publicity / Press Releases
- Personal Communications – Letters
- Personal Communications – Pounding the Pavement
- Word of Mouth - Buzz
- White Papers / Case Studies
- Referrals / Centers of Influence
- Professional Selling
- Networking
- Direct Mail / Postcards
- Newsletters / E-Newsletters
- Direct Faxing
- Telemarketing
- Advertising - Newspaper
- Advertising - Magazines
- Advertising - Radio
- Advertising – Television

- Yellow Pages / Directories
- Promotions / Specials / Giveaways / Contests
- Web Sites
- Banner Ads
- Search Engines
- Direct Email – Opt In
- Direct Email – Spamming
- Conventions / Tradeshows
- Billboards / Sporting Events
- Retail Signage
- Vehicle / Transportation Signs
- Network Marketing
- Point of Sale / Packaging
- Card Decks
- Infomercials
- Audios, Videos, CDs
- Catalogs / Brochures
- Fax on Demand
- Speeches / Articles

IDENTIFY THE WAYS YOU HAVE DELIVERED MESSAGES TO CUSTOMERS

Of the methods you have used to deliver messages to customers (see former page), which have been most successful for getting through to your customers? Rank the top ten in order of importance / success (with 1 being your MOST successful method). (pp 157 – 161)

1.

2.

3.

4.

5.

6.

7.

8.

9.

10.

IDENTIFY SUCCESSFUL METHODS FOR CUSTOMER COMMUNICATIONS

Of the successful methods listed on the previous page, how can you INCREASE, FURTHER DEVELOP, or BETTER LEVERAGE those successful methods? (When something works, you must study it, and learn how to repeat and increase it.) (pp 157 – 161)

REPEAT AND INCREASE SUCCESSFUL CUSTOMER COMMUNICATION METHODS

As you look at your industry, which ways of communicating with customers are the most commonly used? List the top 10. (pp 157 – 161)

1.

2.

3.

4.

5.

6.

7.

8.

9.

10.

STUDY THE INDUSTRY TO IDENTIFY CUSTOMER COMMUNICATIONS METHODS

Study those customer communications methods used by your industry. Which ones are intriguing to you? Which should you consider using? (The tenant in advertising is that only successful methods are repeated and used regularly. While it is not always true, in general, if someone uses a method repeatedly over the course of time, it is probably working for them.) (pp 157 – 161)

CONSIDER HOW YOU MIGHT USE METHODS USED BY THE INDUSTRY

Frequency relates to repeating the same messages to your prospective customers. This repetition is almost always necessary to develop a business. Describe how the concept of frequency impacts your marketing approach? (pp 161 – 166)

STUDY HOW FREQUENCY IMPACTS YOUR BUSINESS

One of the best suggestions for selecting the "right" method to deliver messages is to use several different ways to deliver similar messages (i.e. combining direct mail with telephone follow up, and in-person visits). How do you incorporate a multitude of different ways to deliver customer messages? (pp 157 – 161)

USE MULTIPLE WAYS TO DELIVER MESSAGES

Describe how you utilize a "frequency based sequence" of communications? What are the advantages of this approach for you? (pp 157 – 161)

USE A FREQUENCY-BASED SERIES OF COMMUNICATIONS

In advertising terms, "reach" describes how many people are exposed to a given message. How does the concept of reach impact your marketing communications? (pp 157 – 161)

STUDY HOW "REACH" IMPACTS YOUR BUSINESS

What are five ways you could better utilize your daily communications (things you are already doing and paying for) to better deliver or reinforce your marketing messages? (pp 166)

1.

2.

3.

4.

5.

MAXIMIZE DAILY COMMUNICATIONS

In many instances, some of the best marketing techniques are inexpensive or even free. (They usually require creativity and effort.) What are seven ways you could increase the use of low-cost or no-cost marketing communications strategies? How can you look for inexpensive marketing approaches versus trying to throw money at it? (pp 166 –167)

1.

2.

3.

4.

5.

6.

7.

FIND NO-COST AND LOW-COST COMMUNICATION APPROACHES

How do you measure the success of your customer communications program? How can you quantify return on investment for these activities? (pp 169 – 172)

STUDY THE RESULTS OF YOUR COMMUNICATIONS EFFORTS

What are the steps you take to evaluate, revise, and improve your customer communications approach? List five ways you can do this. (pp 169 – 172)

1.

2.

3.

4.

5.

REVISE AND ADAPT YOUR COMMUNICATIONS APPROACH

How can you create value for your customers during the process of delivering customer communications? How can your messages help them or make their lives better or easier? What can you do to make your customer communications helpful instead of just promotive? (pp 172 – 173)

LOOK FOR WAYS TO CREATE VALUE WITH YOUR CUSTOMER COMMUNICATIONS

Customers are busy. Often, some of the best customer communications can be around reminding customers about your company and that they need to buy. How can you incorporate the concept of reminders into your customer communications approach? What might customers forget that you need them to remember? List five ways. (pp 173 – 174)

1.

2.

3.

4.

5.

USE REMINDERS IN CUSTOMER COMMUNICATIONS

Every industry has a logical way which customers learn about companies, their products, and the normal shopping patterns they go through. What are the logical ways that customers come to make purchases in your industry? How can you walk backwards from the purchase and study how the customer comes to know your company and why to purchase from you?

STUDY THE NORMAL WAY CUSTOMERS GAIN INFORMATION ABOUT PURCHASING IN YOUR INDUSTRY

It is rare that you communicate with a customer once and they immediately buy what you are selling. In the sales process, persistence often plays an important role. Describe four ways that you use persistence in your customer communications approach?

1.

2.

3.

4.

INCORPORATE PERSISTENCE IN YOUR COMMUNICATIONS APPROACH

People who sell advertising can be an incredible resource for learning about what their approaches can do to help you. As well, vendors sell to others in your industry and have an understanding of best practices. Demand that your media reps and vendors become a resource for your company. What can you learn from media reps regarding customer communications? What can you learn from vendor sales reps regarding best industry practices regarding customer communications?

USE YOUR VENDORS AND THEIR REPS AS A RESOURCE

How do you use creative services to facilitate your communications approach? How could you enhance this? (pp 174 – 175)

USE CREATIVE SERVICES TO IMPROVE YOUR COMMUNICATIONS

How can you avoid the temptation of getting bored with your own customer communications? How will you know when you need to cease being consistent with your approach and change things up at the right time? (pp 175)

IF IT IS WORKING, KEEP DOING IT

How do you ask for the sale in customer communications? Have you incorporated closing techniques into your approach? Could you do more of this? (pp 175 – 176)

ASK FOR THE SALE IN YOUR CUSTOMER COMMUNICATIONS

Describe how the M-Cubed (Message, Method / Media, Measurement) relates to the growth of your business.

STUDY HOW THE M-CUBED METHOD IMPACTS YOUR BUSINESS

List ten ways you could improve your customer communications.

1.

2.

3.

4.

5.

6.

7.

8.

9.

10.

STUDY HOW TO IMPROVE YOUR CUSTOMER COMMUNICATIONS

PILLAR 7

MANAGE EXPECTATIONS BRILLIANTLY

PILLAR 7: MANAGE EXPECTATIONS BRILLIANTLY

Customers only give your company their hard earned money if they have an expectation they will be getting something very positive in return. These expectations, coupled with the customer's perception of how you performed in relation to them, determine if the customer leaves the transaction happy. Thus, it also determines if they will be back, become loyal fans of your business, and if they will tell their friends positive things about you. Your image, and ultimately the longevity of your business, is determined by a successful approach to managing expectations such that customers are satisfied with your company.

Describe seven ways you currently exceed the expectations of your customers. (pp 180)

1.

2.

3.

4.

5.

6.

7.

KNOW HOW YOU EXCEED CUSTOMER EXPECTATIONS

Properly managing and exceeding customer expectations have significant advantages for the business. What are five significant advantages your company will derive by exceeding customer expectations? (pp 180 – 183)

1.

2.

3.

4.

5.

IDENTIFY THE SPECIFIC ADVANTAGES EXCEEDING EXPECTATIONS HAS FOR YOU

What are seven significant disadvantages your company will have if you fail to live up to customer expectations? What impact will this have on your long-term future? (pp 180 – 183)

1.

2.

3.

4.

5.

6.

7.

KNOW THE DISADVANTAGES OF FAILING TO EXCEED EXPECTATIONS

How loyal are your customers? In what ways has this been impacted by your ability to exceed their expectations? How can you improve? (pp 180 – 183)

ASSESS THE LOYALTY CUSTOMERS SHOW YOU

In your company, what is the relationship between how well you perform with customers and your image / reputation in the marketplace? (pp 180 – 183)

EXPECTATIONS MANAGEMENT IMPACTS YOUR IMAGE

In what ways does exceeding customer expectations impact the forward momentum of your business? What are five strategies you could implement to improve this in your business? (pp 180 – 183)

1.

2.

3.

4.

5.

EXCEED EXPECTATIONS TO FUEL FORWARD MOMENTUM

How do your employees react to customer satisfaction or dissatisfaction? In what ways does this impact their personal job satisfaction level? How could you use this to improve company morale? (pp 180 – 183)

EXCEEDING CUSTOMER EXPECTATIONS BOOSTS EMPLOYEE MORALE

List five instances where your company failed to exceed customer expectations. What went wrong? What can you learn from this? (pp 180 – 183)

1.

2.

3.

4.

5.

ASSESS INSTANCES WHERE YOU FAILED TO EXCEED CUSTOMER EXPECTATIONS AND LEARN FROM THIS

There is a real dollar cost associated with losing a customer - and this amount can be calculated. Studying this can provide insight into the importance of great expectations management. What is your direct financial cost of losing a customer? (pp 180 – 183)

QUANTIFY THE DOLLAR COST OF LOSING A CUSTOMER

Can you list three circumstances where failing to satisfy customers negatively impacted your personal satisfaction with the business? What could you do differently? (pp 180 – 183)

1.

2.

3.

IMPROVE YOUR PERSONAL SATISFACTION BY DOING WELL WITH CUSTOMERS

The CUSTOMER PILLARS book highlights a 5-Step process to Expectations Management.

5-STEP EXPECTATIONS MANAGEMENT PROCESS

1. Understand base expectations

2. Influence expectations

3. Product / service performance

4. The company experience

5. Post-purchase follow up

In what ways are you currently using the 5-Step Method to Expectations Management in your business? What is working extremely well? What isn't? (pp 184 – 186)

ASSESS THE WAYS YOU ARE CURRENTLY USING THE 5-STEP PROCESS

Are there steps in the five-step method you are under-utilizing or completely ignoring currently? What are seven ways you could better use these steps to your advantage? (pp 184 – 186)

1.

2.

3.

4.

5.

6.

7.

INCREASE YOUR USE OF THE 5-STEP PROCESS

Do you take expectations management in your business as seriously as you should? What are five ways you could increase your own personal commitment to this concept? Do you treat expectations management as a high level management process in addition to it being an employee development approach? (Both are necessary.) (pp 184 – 186)

1.

2.

3.

4.

5.

TAKE EXPECTATIONS MANAGEMENT SERIOUSLY

What are ten of the most significant base expectations customers bring to the interaction with your company before they are even introduced to your business? (pp 184 – 186)

1.

2.

3.

4.

5.

6.

7.

8.

9.

10.

STUDY BASE EXPECTATIONS

In many instances, the base expectations customers bring to the transaction work in our favor; they actually set the stage for success. How do customer base expectations work in your favor in your interactions with them? Do you fully capitalize on these? How could you improve? (pp 184 – 186)

STUDY BASE EXPECTATIONS THAT WORK IN YOUR FAVOR

What base expectations does the customer bring to your interactions that impair your ability to succeed in transactions with them? How do you handle this? (pp 184 – 186)

IDENTIFY BASE EXPECATIONS THAT GET IN THE WAY OF SUCCESS

Where do customers get these base expectations? What insights can you gain by understanding how your customers have learned or been influenced in the past? List five key sources of these base expectations. (pp 184 – 186)

1.

2.

3.

4.

5.

STUDY THE SOURCES OF BASE EXPECTATIONS

In what ways does the industry or your competitors impact the base expectations customers have? How does this work in your favor? To your detriment? How can you use this to your advantage? List seven ways. (pp 184 – 186)

1.

2.

3.

4.

5.

6.

7.

THE INDUSTRY IMPACTS BASE EXPECTATIONS

When customers bring expectations that cannot be fulfilled, we are actually set up to fail. (If the expectations can't be met, and we know this going in and we do nothing, we know the customer will not be happy.) What expectations do customers have that are unrealistic? How will you deal with this? List five. (pp 184 – 186)

1.

2.

3.

4.

5.

UNREALISTIC BASE EXPECTATIONS MUST BE ADDRESSED

Other times, the customer comes with low expectations. (Easy to achieve, but this may make them apathetic to the purchase.) Which base expectations need to be adjusted upwards through your customer communications? What are your goals pertaining to modifying these expectations? List three. (pp 184 – 186)

1.

2.

3.

SOME BASE EXPECTATIONS NEED TO BE RAISED

Promises to the market are tricky. Promise too much, and you set yourself up to perform under expectations. Promise too little and the customer may not be interested in doing business. This is a delicate balance. Describe how your promises are sufficiently high to excite the market, yet low enough that you can exceed them with consistency? How does this dynamic impact your business? (pp 184 – 186)

MAKE THE RIGHT PROMISES TO THE MARKET

When we interact with customers, we impact their expectations. Describe five ways your current customer communications impact customer expectations? Do they appropriately modify (up or down) expectations? Do your communications make the right promises? (pp 190 – 192)

1.

2.

3.

4.

5.

CRAFT MARKETING MESSAGES TO APPROPRIATELY INFLUENCE EXPECTATIONS

Describe a time when you over-promised to the market? What was the result? What did you learn from this situation? (pp 190 – 192)

LEARN FROM AN INSTANCE WHERE YOU OVERPROMISED

What are the results when you see a competitor over-promise to customers? Did this backfire? Was it the case of short-term gains accompanied by long-term loss? (pp 190 – 192)

LEARN FROM AN INSTANCE WHERE A COMPETITOR OVERPROMISED

Do the commitments you make to customers set you up to succeed or to fail? Describe. (pp 190 – 192)

SET YOURSELF UP TO SUCCEED WITH EXPECTATIONS

What are five components of the ideal promises you need to make to customers? How do you communicate these? (pp 190 – 192)

1.

2.

3.

4.

5.

DEEPLY STUDY THE RIGHT PROMISES TO MAKE TO CUSTOMERS

List 3 changes you need to make to your customer communications approach in order to set better expectations. (pp 190 – 192)

1.

2.

3.

MODIFY YOUR COMMUNICATIONS TO SET BETTER EXPECTATIONS

How does the current design of your product or service impact the level of satisfaction customers have with your company? Does it exceed their expectations? Are there improvements that would help this? (pp 193 – 195)

ENSURE YOUR PRODUCT OR SERVICE IS DESIGNED TO EXCEED EXPECTATIONS

Quality is talked about extensively in many companies and, certainly, this does impact expectations management. But too many companies discuss quality in terms that are too vague. If you are going to exceed expectations based on quality, be very specific about the quality points which impact customers. What are the seven key quality points of your product or service that most impact the way customers judge your performance in relation to their expectations? (pp 193 – 195)

1.

2.

3.

4.

5.

6.

7.

BE SPECIFIC ABOUT WHICH QUALITY POINTS MOST IMPACT CUSTOMERS

Customers will often tell us if our products or services do not live up to their expectations. They do this in the form of complaints. (Remember MOST people will not complain, but will be disappointed without telling you. When people complain it is a MAJOR opportunity to learn.) How do you track quality complaints? Are you sufficiently learning from these comments? How could you gain more from complaints? (pp 193 – 195)

LEARN FROM COMPLAINTS

Most employees are not fully able to handle complaints without training from your company. How have you trained your staff to be able to take complaints in a way that customers appreciate, as well as that garners the insights complaints can provide? What additional training should you provide your staff in the area of appropriately handling complaints? (pp 193 – 195)

TRAIN YOUR EMPLOYEES TO BEST HANDLE COMPLAINTS

What systems do you have in place so you can learn from positive comments you receive from customers when you exceed their expectations? Is there a way you could formalize this important process? (pp 193 – 195)

LEARN FROM POSTITIVE FEEDBACK

What research do you conduct on the front end to ensure your products or services will exceed expectations when they are brought to market? Are there additional ways you could market test? (pp 193 – 195)

DO FRONT END RESEARCH TO UNDERSTAND HOW YOUR PRODUCT EXCEEDS EXPECTATIONS

Often products and services must be modified or improved to ensure they greatly exceed customer expectations. Do you need to make any revisions to your product or service offering to improve how they perform in relation to customer expectations? List five. (pp 193 – 195)

1.

2.

3.

4.

5.

IMPROVE YOUR PRODUCT TO EXCEED EXPECTATIONS

If you were to rank yourself and your company on a scale of 1 to 10, how well do you listen to customers? List five ways you could listen more. (pp. 198 – 202)

1.

2.

3.

4.

5.

LISTEN TO CUSTOMERS

Complaints can be an opportunity to answer the customer's concern so well that they are converted to customers for life. List five ways you could capitalize on this. (pp. 198 – 202)

1.

2.

3.

4.

5.

CONVERT COMPLAINERS INTO CUSTOMERS FOR LIFE

In many industries, service is the distinction. Winning or losing comes down to being very easy and pleasurable to do business with. What are ten things you could do in your company to makes it easy and pleasurable to do business with you? (pp. 198 – 202)

1.

2.

3.

4.

5.

6.

7.

8.

9.

10.

MAKE IT VERY EASY TO DO BUSINESS WITH YOU

Time is a huge factor in today's world. Many industries have been created simply on making things faster and more convenient. What are five steps you could take that would make it significantly more convenient or save time for customers? (pp. 198 – 202)

1.

2.

3.

4.

5.

FOCUS ON CUSTOMER CONVENIENCE AND SPEED

Hey, live it up a little! Having fun in your business not only translates into better relationships with customers, but also significantly enhances the experience employees have with your company. What are three shifts you could make in the business that would make doing business with you more fun or entertaining? (pp. 198 – 202)

1.

2.

3.

MAKE IT FUN TO DO BUSINESS WITH YOU

Pleasant surprises can be an excellent marketing tactic. Catching customers off guard and doing something very positive, yet unexpected can build a significant business. What are five things you could do in your business that would pleasantly surprise customers? What positive things could you do that the customer would not be expecting? What steps will you need to take to "wow" your customers? (pp. 198 – 202)

1.

2.

3.

4.

5.

LOOK FOR WAYS TO PLEASANTLY SURPRISE YOUR CUSTOMERS

What are 20 details that would comprise the ideal experience a customer would have with your company? How far is the actual experience from this perfect situation? What would it take for you to close this gap? (pp. 196 - 198)

1.

2.

3.

4.

5.

6.

7.

8.

9.

10.

11.

12.

13.

14.

15.

16.

17.

18.

19.

20.

CREATE THE IDEAL CUSTOMER EXPERIENCE

Often what you hope the customer experience will be and what it actually is can be two very different things. One of the contributing factors to this is poor employee training. What are ten employee training steps you take to ensure the customer's experience with your company is consistent each time they interact with your business? How could you improve? (pp. 196 - 198)

1.

2.

3.

4.

5.

6.

7.   .

8.

9.

10.

TRAIN YOUR EMPLOYEES TO CREATE THE IDEAL CUSTOMER EXPERIENCE

The following is a list of traditional customer service elements. Describe how these impact your company and make a list of ten ways you could improve. (pp 198 – 202)

SERVICE ELEMENTS

- Convenience
- Save time
- Have fun
- The right attitude
- Listen
- Promptness
- Cleanliness
- Professionalism
- Trust
- Responsibility
- Competency
- Surprise them

1.

2.

3.

4.

5.

6.

7.

8.

9.

10.

USE TRADITIONAL CUSTOMER SERVICE ELEMENTS TO YOUR ADVANTAGE

Communicating with customers after the purchase is a seldom used marketing tactic. (But an important one!) How do you use post-purchase follow up with your customers today? What are the procedures you have in place to communicate with customers after their purchase to gauge their satisfaction level with your company? List seven ways you could increase your post-purchase follow up. (pp 206 – 209)

1.

2.

3.

4.

5.

6.

7.

USE POST-PURCHASE FOLLOW UP TO EHANCE EXPECTATIONS MANAGEMENT

How could post-purchase follow up significantly impact your ongoing revenues from customers? What do you need to do to take advantage of this tool in your business? (pp 206 – 209)

ENHANCE REVENUES WITH POST-PURCHASE FOLLOW UP

It has been said that employees will never treat customers better than their employer treats them as an employee. How does this impact your business? List five ways you could improve. (pp 209 – 212)

1.

2.

3.

4.

5.

TREAT EMPLOYEES THE WAY YOU WANT THEM TO TREAT YOUR CUSTOMERS

Can you think of an instance when you or someone in your business lost a customer over a trivial dispute? What did you learn from that circumstance? Was it worth it? Can you use this in training employees on the value of retaining customers? (pp 209 – 212)

KEEP PERSPECTIVE – DON'T LOSE A CUSTOMER OVER LITTLE THINGS

One great way to improve in expectations management is to take a problem area and OVER-FIX it. This means taking what was previously a weakness and turning it into a serious strength. It also means solving the problem once and for all. Tackle the problem with a vengeance! List a common problem you have in an area relating to expectations management. Then list ten things you could do to over-fix the problem. (pp 209 – 212)

Describe the common problem:

Ten steps you could take to over-fix it:

1.

2.

3.

4.

5.

6.

7.

8.

9.

10.

OVERFIX PROBLEMS SO THEY GO AWAY FOR GOOD AND BECOME STRENGTHS

Are your policies and procedures set up for the 97% of customers that are honest and good, or the 3% that will try to take advantage of you? Describe. Are your policies customer-friendly or are they punitive? How do you bring this more into your long-term favor? (pp 209 – 212)

POLICIES AND PROCEDURES SHOULD ENHANCE CUSTOMER RELATIONSHIPS

How have you studied lost or angry customers in the past? What did you learn? How can you use this to a greater degree in the future? List seven things you have learned from upset or angry customers. (pp 209 – 212)

1.

2.

3.

4.

5.

6.

7.

LEARN FROM UPSET CUSTOMERS

Secret shoppers are customers who are set up more to evaluate your business (from a customer's perspective) than they are to actually purchase. In a way this is "spying on your business", but the goal is to capture an unbiased, accurate reflection of how customers view your company. How could you incorporate secret shoppers to better learn how customers truly react to your company and its employee? List seven things you would like to learn (questions you would like to answer). (pp 212)

1.

2.

3.

4.

5.

6.

7.

USE SECRET SHOPPERS TO GAIN INSIGHT ON
HOW CUSTOMERS REALLY PERCEIVE YOUR BUSINESS

How you manage and exceed customer expectations could very well be the most important key to your ongoing success. List ten ways you will enhance your expectations management strategies.

1.

2.

3.

4.

5.

6.

7.

8.

9.

10.

MANAGE EXPECTATIONS BRILLIANTLY

PILLAR 8

LEARN FROM THE MARKET

PILLAR 8: LEARN FROM THE MARKET

Growing a company is no easy task. If you talk to the most successful companies, they will tell you they have made and learned from many mistakes along the way. Studying your successes and failures, the market, and how it reacts to your company is an important part of the evolution of a company. Being successful is not about sitting down, being real smart, and figuring it out all at once. It just doesn't work that way. There's an element of experimentation and refinement and the faster you can learn, the faster you will meet your objectives. Take a humble student and serious learning approach to running your business.

What are the ten most important things you have learned about your customers and the markets you are serving? What impact has this additional information had on your business? (pp 216 – 220)

1.

2.

3.

4.

5.

6.

7.

8.

9.

10.

STUDY WHAT YOU HAVE LEARNED ABOUT CUSTOMERS

There are many ways to learn about customers and the markets you serve. What are the main ways / sources you have learned from and about the markets? (pp 216 – 220)

KNOW HOW YOU LEARN ABOUT MARKETS

How important is learning about your customers in your business? If you could "figure out" your market, what impact would that have on your success? What value does the "humble student" approach have for your company? (pp 218 – 220)

THERE IS GREAT VALUE AT INCREASING YOUR MARKET KNOWLEDGE

Central to evolving your business is adapting and modifying your approach. No one starts out their business with a firm idea of how success will be achieved and then never deviates from that plan. Good businesses observe what works, what doesn't, and then take corrective steps based on their new knowledge. List five ways you have adapted, modified, or refined your approach to growing your business. (pp 222 – 224)

1.

2.

3.

4.

5.

REFINE, ADAPT, IMPROVE, MODIFY

One key to learning from the market is to be specific about the knowledge you seek. What are ten key things you would like to learn from the market, questions you would like to answer, or assumptions you would like to confirm about the market and your customers? (pp 220 – 221)

1.

2.

3.

4.

5.

6.

7.

8.

9.

10.

KNOW THE KEY QUESTIONS YOU WOULD LIKE ANSWERED

Marketing research doesn't have to be overly complicated; in fact, it can be quite informal. How do you use informal conversations and questioning with customers to learn about their preferences and how to better market to them? (pp 233 – 234)

USE INFORMAL CONVERSATION AS A TOOL TO LEARN ABOUT CUSTOMERS

There are lessons in the business everyday. Too often, we observe them, then quickly forget. It is good to record your observations. What methods do you have in place for you and your employees to record key observations you make about the behavior and preferences of your customers? Do you have procedures in place to capture insights as you notice them? How can you improve? (pp 234)

PUT PROCESSES IN PLACE TO RECORD OBSERVATIONS ABOUT CUSTOMERS

What are ten things you are either measuring or could measure that would provide meaningful insight into the forward progression of your business? What are the important metrics in your business? What do you (or could you) learn from monitoring them more closely? (pp 224 – 228)

1.

2.

3.

4.

5.

6.

7.

8.

9.

10.

IDENTIFY KEY MEASUREMENT ITEMS TO MONITOR IN YOUR BUSINESS

Every company keeps records. In many instances, these records contain great marketing insights, if they are harvested out of the numbers. In what ways do you use your customer database or your financials to learn about what is going on with customers? List five key ways. (pp 224 – 228)

1.

2.

3.

4.

5.

USE YOUR FINANCIALS AND YOUR DATABASE TO GAIN CUSTOMER KNOWLEDGE

Every business tries things that do not work. (When you hear people brag that they have never made a business mistake, know you are dealing with someone who is not in touch with reality!) Failures in marketing are often the impetus for finding great solutions. In what ways have you learned from failed experiments in the business? How could you use this to your advantage? List three circumstances. (pp 222 – 223)

1.

2.

3.

LEARN FROM FAILED EXPERIMENTS

It has been said that the best way to succeed in business is to test things small. That way if they do not work, you do not suffer too much and have the ability to adapt and try something different. Do you test new things such that if the experiment is not successful, you will be okay? How can you adopt a learning approach to experimenting within your business? (pp 222 – 224)

TEST THINGS SMALL, THEN LEVERAGE SUCCESSES AND MODIFY FAILURES

List ten ways that you use the Internet to collect information about customers and the market. What are ten additional ways you could use the Internet to learn and better put your company in a position for success? (pp 229 – 230)

Ways You Currently Use the Internet	Ways You Could Use the Internet

USE THE INTERNET TO LEARN ABOUT CUSTOMERS

There is a great deal of information already available which can help you with learning about your customers. How could you use the following to learn more about your business? (pp 229 – 232)

Your public library:

Industry associations:

Industry reports:

Your local Small Business Development Center (SBDC):

TAP INTO KEY INFORMATION RESOURCES

Marketing research can be expensive. However, there are dozens of ways to learn about customers and the overall market which cost very little or nothing. List six cheap ways you could learn about your market and what you would need to do so. (pp 233 – 237)

1.

2.

3.

4.

5.

6.

LOOK FOR CHEAP WAYS TO LEARN ABOUT CUSTOMERS

How have you studied the ways your competitors communicate with customers? What insights have you gained from this? How could you do more of this?

LEARN FROM COMPETITOR'S COMMUNICATION APPROACHES

Have you incorporated more formal marketing research into your approach? How could you use these techniques without breaking the bank? Some common ways are listed below. How might they apply? (pp 233 – 237)

- Shop the competition

- Customer's junk mail

- Tradeshows

- Vendors

- Customer roundtables

- Web-based research

- Surveys / questionnaires

- Secret shoppers

- Soft launch / beta testing

- Moderated discussions – one-on-one or focus group

CONSIDER WAYS TO EFFECTIVELY USE MORE FORMAL RESEARCH

What steps do you take in your research with customers to ensure you are getting objective, honest information, not biased, inaccurate information? (pp 239 – 240)

TAKE STEPS TO ENSURE YOUR RESEARCH IS OBJECTIVE

In some situations, research can be used as a "foot in the door" selling technique. This must be done with caution (and not be manipulative). Are there appropriate ways for you to use research as a selling tool? Describe them. (pp 240 – 241)

WHEN APPROPRIATE, USE RESEARCH AS PART OF A SELLING APPROACH

What are ten ways you can better "learn from the market?"

1.

2.

3.

4.

5.

6.

7.

8.

9.

10.

LEARN FROM THE MARKET

PILLAR 9

PRACTICE COORDINATED GROWTH PLANNING

PILLAR 9: PRACTICE COORDINATED GROWTH PLANNING

These pillars do not operate independent of each other. They all work together to determine how a company evolves. Planning how to integrate the various components of these pillars is important. But it doesn't stop there: the approach to customer / revenues development must be coordinated with many other elements in the business to ensure that some of the common pitfalls of expansion are avoided. Additionally, "big picture" strategic plans must be boiled down into tactical, "things to do" lists so that big ideas can be implemented and actually realized. True success is rarely an accident, and planning helps put you in a better position to capitalize on the opportunities which come your way. Don't leave growth to chance!

The advantages of strategic growth planning are many. Based on your business, what are five major advantages you would receive from excellent strategic growth planning? Are these things significant? (pp 247 – 250)

1.

2.

3.

4.

5.

CONSIDER THE ADVANTAGES OF STRATEGIC GROWTH PLANNING

If you're like most people, you probably do not already use planning to its fullest advantage. What are the hesitancies / concerns you have regarding planning? How might you overcome these things to better embrace the planning process? (pp 247 – 250)

LOOK AT WHY YOU MIGHT BE RELUCTANT TO PLAN AND HOW TO GET OVER IT

One of the goals of planning is to save time (that incredibly precious commodity in the business!). What impact would planning have on your own personal time? List ten ways planning could save you time. (pp 247 – 248)

1.

2.

3.

4.

5.

6.

7.

8.

9.

10.

STUDY HOW PLANNING CAN SAVE YOU TIME

The *CUSTOMER PILLARS* book describes success in business as the careful coordination of a thousand small variables instead of one major issue. How does this concept impact your business? How can you use this perspective to your advantage? (pp 244 – 246)

MARKETING SUCCESS IS THE COORDINATION OF 1,000 VARIABLES

How could you use the nine principles from the *CUSTOMER PILLARS* system as your basis for strategic growth planning? How will you use this system for planning in your business? (pp 250 – 252)

USE THE *CUSTOMER PILLARS* TO ORGANIZE CUSTOMER MANAGEMENT

List ten mind maps you could do that will help you with clarifying your strategic situation. There are three blank mind maps attached. For more information about mind mapping techniques, see the books by Tony Buzan, the inventor and guru on the topic. (pp 250 – 252)

1.

2.

3.

4.

5.

6.

7.

8.

9.

10.

USE MINDMAPS AS A POWERFUL PLANNING TOOL

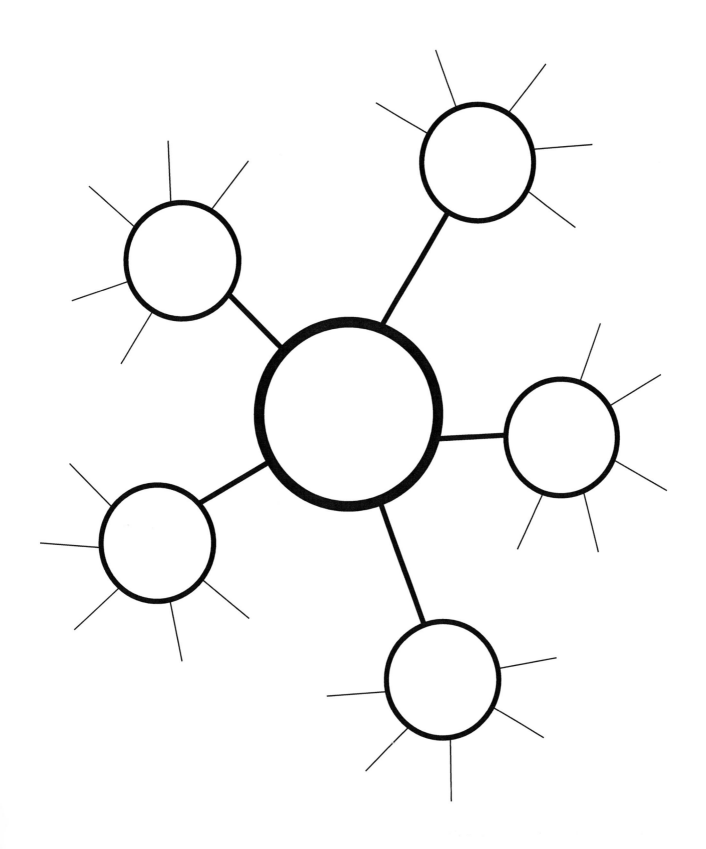

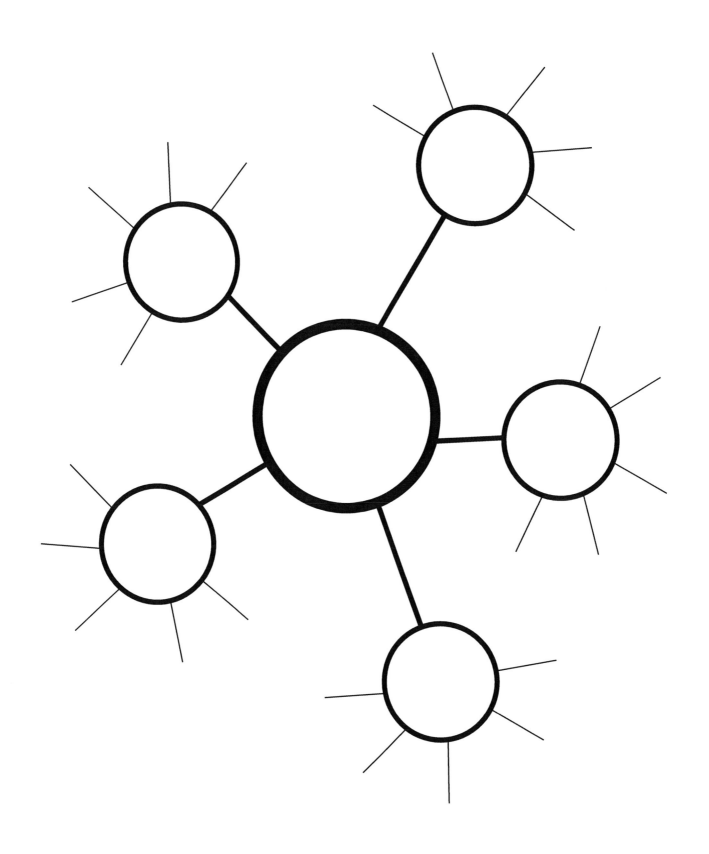

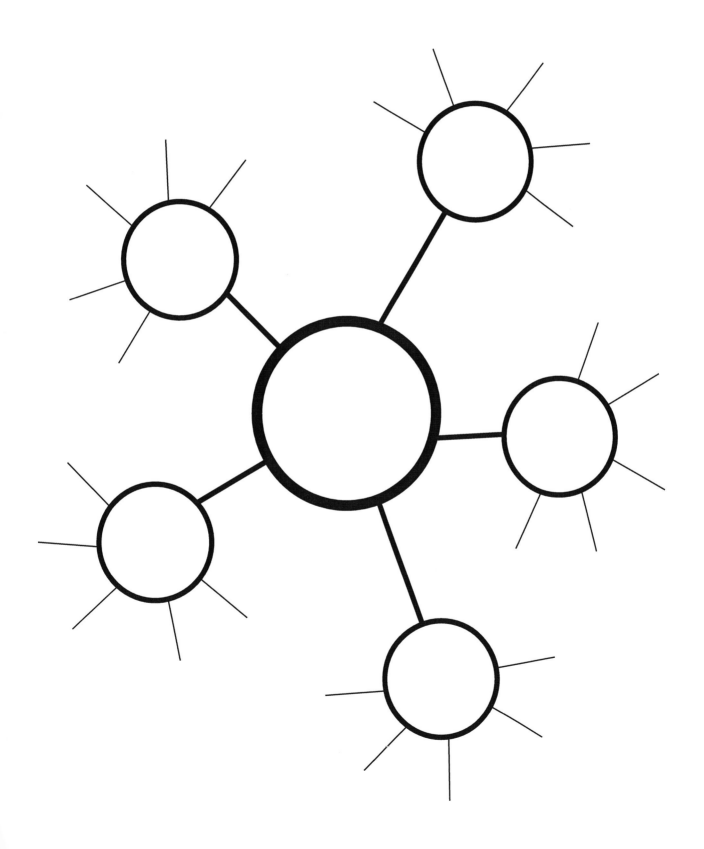

A great planning exercise is to study your business by revenue streams. What are the three to eight different revenue streams within your business? Which streams are you the most excited about? What is your current mix between the different revenue streams? What is your ideal mix? How are your expansion efforts supporting your desired changes in revenue streams? (pp 252 – 254)

Revenue Stream	Outlook	Current %	Desired %	Desired Changes

CONSIDER PLANNING IN TERMS OF REVENUE STREAMS

In addition, look at the same revenue streams in financial/numeric terms. (pp 252 – 254)

Revenue Stream	$ Size of Average Sale	Margin %	Margin Trend	Estimated Number of Customers

LOOK AT THE FINANCIAL IMPACTS OF REVENUE STREAMS

When you look at your strategic growth plan, is it completely consistent with the overall direction of the business? If you achieve your goals, will this be the right move for the company? (pp 256 – 258)

CONFIRM THAT YOUR REVENUE GOALS ARE CONSISTENT WITH THE OVERALL BUSINESS

Revenue growth has an impact on each of the functions within the business (marketing, finance, accounting, human resources, etc). What potential problems can the anticipated expansion create for these other functions? What support do you need from each of these other functions in order to succeed with the business development effort? (Note: this is true even in very small companies, there may not be different people or departments responsible for these functions, but in every business the different functions are present.) (pp 256 – 258)

MARKETING / SALES DEPARTMENT:

OPERATIONS DEPARTMENT:

RESEARCH & DEVELOPMENT / PRODUCT DEVELOPMENT:

SHIPPING DEPARTMENT:

PURCHASING DEPARTMENT:

ACCOUNTING DEPARTMENT:

FINANCE DEPARTMENT:

HUMAN RESOURCES DEPARTMENT:

TRAINING DEPARTMENT:

INFORMATION TECHNOLOGY DEPARTMENT:

STRATEGIC PLANNING DEPARTMENT:

OVERALL MANAGEMENT:

OTHER FUNCTIONS:

CLOSELY CONSIDER THE IMPACTS GROWTH WILL HAVE ON OTHER FUNCTIONS (OR DEPARTMENTS) AND THE SUPPORT YOU WILL NEED FROM THEM

There are possible pitfalls to growth. Careless and ill-planned growth can be disastrous for a company. Listed below are some of the common errors that can accompany growth. Discuss how you have prepared to avoid the possible pitfalls of development? (pp 258 – 263)

THE POSSIBLE PITFALLS OF GROWTH

- Revenues grow, but profits shrink
- Sacrificing margins to grow revenues
- Failing to understand cash requirements of growth
- Poor inventory management
- Poor receivables management
- Sacrificing long-term growth for short-term gains
- Growth at any cost
- Growth that cannot be fulfilled
- Expenses occur but growth does not
- Growth with the wrong customers
- Growth that decreases quality
- Growth that is not synergistic

PREPARE TO AVOID THE POSSIBLE DOWNSIDES OF GROWTH

Specifically, one of the possible downsides of growth is a crunch of cash resources (especially early in the developmental process and if you have inventory and receivables). What are the cash ramifications of your expected development? Have you completed written cashflow projections (see next page)? Do you have the cash reserves to support the anticipated expansion? Discuss this here. (pp 259 – 260)

CAREFULLY STUDY THE CASH IMPACTS OF GROWTH

Projected CashFlow Analysis
ABC Company

CASHFLOW STATEMENT	Month 1	Month 2	Month 3	Month 4	Month 5	Month 6	Month 7	Month 8	Month 9	Mo 10	Mo 11	Mo 12	YEAR 1	YEAR 2	YEAR 3
STARTING CASH BALANCE	0	35,990	31,780	29,770	31,860	35,150	39,640	38,530	39,420	35,310	41,600	49,690	0	57,180	75,190
SOURCES OF CASH															
Revenue Stream 1	7,000	8,000	11,000	12,000	15,000	15,000	18,000	17,000	15,000	25,000	20,000	18,000	181,000	222,000	277,500
Revenue Stream 2	2,000	4,000	8,000	8,000	12,000	14,000	10,000	6,000	8,000	7,000	15,000	16,000	110,000	155,000	175,000
Collection of Accounts Recv	4,000	2,000	2,000	2,000	2,000	2,000	2,000	2,000	2,000	2,000	2,000	2,000	26,000	3,000	3,000
Other 1	0	0	0	0	0	0	0	0	0	0	0	0	0	0	0
Other 2	0	0	0	0	0	0	0	0	0	0	0	0	0	0	0
Cash Received from Loans	65,000	0	0	0	0	0	0	0	0	0	0	0	65,000	0	0
Owners' Cash Capital Injections	20,000	0	0	0	0	0	0	0	0	0	0	0	20,000	0	0
TOTAL CASH INFLOWS	98,000	14,000	21,000	22,000	29,000	31,000	30,000	25,000	25,000	34,000	37,000	36,000	402,000	380,000	455,500
Direct Inventory Replenishment	3,600	4,800	7,600	8,000	10,800	11,600	11,200	9,200	9,200	12,800	14,000	13,600	116,400	150,800	181,000
Change in Inventory Levels	40,000	0	0	0	0	0	0	0	5,000	0	0	0	45,000	5,000	5,000
Salaries / Benefits	5,000	5,000	7,000	7,000	10,000	10,000	10,000	10,000	10,000	10,000	10,000	10,000	104,000	125,000	150,000
Rent	1,800	1,800	1,800	1,800	1,800	1,800	1,800	1,800	1,800	1,800	1,800	1,800	21,600	22,800	24,000
Utilities	300	300	300	300	300	300	300	300	300	300	300	300	3,600	4,320	5,184
Repairs / Maintenance	50	50	50	50	50	50	50	50	50	50	50	50	600	600	600
Advertising	2,000	2,000	2,000	500	500	500	500	500	500	500	500	500	10,500	12,000	15,000
Commissions	0	0	0	0	0	0	0	0	0	0	0	0	0	0	0
Travel / Entertainment	50	50	50	50	50	50	50	50	50	50	50	50	600	800	1,000
Mailing Costs	50	50	50	50	50	50	50	50	50	50	50	50	600	650	700
Office Supplies	100	100	100	100	100	100	100	100	100	100	100	100	1,200	1,500	1,500
Professional Services	150	150	150	150	150	150	150	150	150	150	150	150	1,800	2,000	2,200
Insurance	100	100	100	100	100	100	100	100	100	100	100	100	1,200	1,500	2,000
Telephone / Internet	100	100	100	100	100	100	100	100	100	100	100	100	1,200	1,500	2,000
Security System	50	50	50	50	50	50	50	50	50	50	50	50	600	600	600
Lease hold Improvements	5,000	0	0	0	0	0	0	0	0	0	0	0	5,000	0	0
Loan Repayment	1,100	1,100	1,100	1,100	1,100	1,100	1,100	1,100	1,100	1,100	1,100	1,100	13,200	13,200	13,200
Owner's Draw	0	0	0	0	0	0	0	0	0	0	0	0	0	10,000	10,000
Equipment Lease Expenses	500	500	500	500	500	500	500	500	500	500	500	500	6,000	9,000	12,000
Capital Equipmnt Expenditures	2,000	2,000	2,000	0	0	0	5,000	0	0	0	0	0	11,000	0	0
Other 1	20	20	20	20	20	20	20	20	20	20	20	20	240	240	240
Other 2	20	20	20	20	20	20	20	20	20	20	20	20	240	240	240
Other 3	20	20	20	20	20	20	20	20	20	20	20	20	240	240	240
TOTAL CASH OUTFLOWS	62,010	18,210	23,010	19,910	25,710	26,510	31,110	24,110	29,110	27,710	28,910	28,510	344,820	361,990	426,704
CHANGE IN CASH	35,990	-4,210	-2,010	2,090	3,290	4,490	-1,110	890	-4,110	6,290	8,090	7,490	57,180	18,010	28,796
ENDING CASH BALANCE	35,990	31,780	29,770	31,860	35,150	39,640	38,530	39,420	35,310	41,600	49,690	57,180	57,180	75,190	103,986

"What is the best way to eat an elephant? One bite at a time." This age-old motivational saying has a huge impact on building a business. List ten ways that you have broken (or could break) your strategic, "bigger picture" plans into smaller, tactical, "things to do" actions which show how daily actions support the overall long-term vision of the company? (pp 264 – 265)

1.

2.

3.

4.

5.

6.

7.

8.

9.

10.

BREAK BIG PICTURE IDEAS INTO A SERIES OF SMALLER STEPS

A strong suggestion for organizing your tactical plans is to develop a calendar of key activities necessary to implement your growth program. List key items below, by month, to accomplish your goals. (pp 264 – 265)

JANUARY:

FEBRUARY:

MARCH:

APRIL:

MAY:

JUNE:

JULY:

AUGUST:

SEPTEMBER:

OCTOBER:

NOVEMBER:

DECEMBER:

DEVELOP AND IMPLEMENT A *CUSTOMER PILLARS* CALENDAR

In marketing, generating lots of ideas will probably not be a problem. Implementing them, however, often is. List five steps you will take to ensure you not only have great ides, but that you implement them with precision and consistency? (pp 264 – 265)

1.

2.

3.

4.

5.

IDEAS WITHOUT IMPLMENTATION ARE NOT WORTH MUCH – FOCUS ON PUTTING IDEAS INTO MOTION

Growth never comes easy, you will be tested, and at times, frustrated – how will you be dedicated, disciplined, and persistent in your efforts? (pp 264 – 265)

PERSISTENCE IS A KEY FOR SUCCESS IN BUSINESS

Profitability is central to the long-term success of a business. You spend money with the intention that those dollars will generate a larger amount of money coming back to the business. How does the concept of "Return On Investment"(ROI) impact your expansion plans? How do you increase your ROI mentality? List ten ways. (pp 266)

1.

2.

3.

4.

5.

6.

7.

8.

9.

10.

EXPANSION EFFORTS SHOULD LEAD TO PROFITABILITY

Planning can be considered in multiple time levels. Are you looking at more than one planning time period? Describe how you address each of the following planning levels. (pp 266 – 267)

90 Days:

6 Months:

1 Year:

3 Years:

5 Years:

10 Years:

CONSIDER MULTIPLE PLANNING TIME PERIODS

The business world is fluid and evolves constantly. To carve out a larger niche for yourself, you must place an emphasis on always getting better. List five ways your strategic planning incorporate a commitment to constant and ongoing improvement? (pp 267)

1.

2.

3.

4.

5.

COMMIT TO CONSTANT AND NEVER ENDING IMPROVEMENT

Too often in business, the focus is to improve what is not working well. This is fine; the only problem though, is it tends to emphasize the negative and not give enough credit to what is working well. List seven ways you can celebrate victories and make a big deal of the small wins along the way. (pp 267)

1.

2.

3.

4.

5.

6.

7.

CELEBRATE AND MAKE A BIG DEAL OF SMALL VICTORIES

Progress often occurs in phases. Planning takes this into account and attempts to break bigger goals down into manageable phases. What are the phases of growth you are planning? (pp 267)

Phase 1 Growth:

Phase 2 Growth:

Phase 3 Growth:

Phase 4 Growth:

Phase 5 Growth:

CONSIDER A PHASED APPROACH TO GROWTH

What can you do to create a bigger vision of the expansion goals of your company? Are you playing in a big enough game? What would it look like if you turned it up a bit? (pp 268 – 269)

CREATE A BIGGER VISION OF WHAT YOUR COMPANY COULD BECOME

Based on your knowledge of the *CUSTOMER PILLARS* system, what are the most important 20 things you need to accomplish in the next 90 days? 6 months? Year? Two years? What do you need to get started?

1.

2.

3.

4.

5.

6.

7.

8.

9.

10.

11.

12.

13.

14.

15.

16.

17.

18.

19.

20.

TAKE THE *CUSTOMER PILLARS* SYSTEM
AND PUT IT INTO MOTION IN YOUR BUSINESS

There is a tremendous amount of information covered in the *CUSTOMER PILLARS* system. Review this notebook and highlight the most important ten items you need to do in the next year.

1.

2.

3.

4.

5.

6.

7.

8.

9.

10.

REVIEW THE WORKBOOK AND IDENTIFY KEY ACTION STEPS

STEPS ALONG THE PATH

Congratulations on completing the exercises found in this workbook. You have taken steps that many entrepreneurs fail to address and, in my opinion, have greatly improved your chances of business success. The concepts found in this workbook drive the development of a company. Go make it happen!

If your goal is to build a company, however, the work you do in this area never stops. I hope you take the principals gained in this workbook (and hopefully also in reading the *CUSTOMER PILLARS* book) and make them an integral part of your ongoing management.

So can we help further?

Of course, the best place to learn about this is at our website at www.customerpillars.com. The author of this system has multiple methods to assist you with integrating this management system into your business in an ongoing way. This could include consulting, coaching, retreats, or participating in one of our mastermind groups. Visit the website, then give us a call. We will design a custom program most suitable for your needs, goals, and budget. We want to help you further.

We wish you the best in growing your company. Please contact us about helping you further.

WWW.CUSTOMERPILLARS.COM

CITATIONS, TRADEMARKS, & THOUGHT LEADERS

My guess is most people who write books also like to read them - I am one of those authors. There have been many books, authors, and speakers who have influenced me -- and thus this workbook. I would like to acknowledge them and recommend you look into their work: The E-Myth Revisited (Michael Gerber), Guerilla Marketing (Jay Conrad Levinson), Permission Marketing (Seth Godin), Outrageous Marketing (Joe Spolestra), The 7 Habits of Highly Effective People (Steven Covey), Think and Grow Rich (Napoleon Hill), Profitable Growth is Everyone's Business (Ram Charan), Your Marketing Audit (Hal Groetsch), Confessions of an Advertising Man (David Ogilvy), The Wizard of Ads (Roy Williams), How to Win Friends and Influence People (Dale Carnegie), The Principles of Marketing (Phillip Kotler), Customers For Life (Carl Sewell), Raving Fans (Ken Blanchard and Sheldon Bowles), Principled Profit (Shel Horowitz), and Positioning (Al Ries and Jack Trout). In addition, the following speakers / trainers / consultants have influenced me: Dan Kennedy, Jeff Paul, Jay Abraham, Tony Buzan, Thomas Leonard, Anthony Robbins, Dennis Waitley, Brian Tracy, Zig Ziglar, and John Maxwell. I thank these individuals for sharing their insights and knowledge and for providing myself and many others the foundation to evolve and develop.

ABOUT THE AUTHOR

Curt Clinkinbeard helps entrepreneurs everyday.

He is the President of Strive Coaching Inc, a consulting, speaking, and publishing business. In his work, he has the opportunity to interact with a wide variety of entrepreneurs around building profitable revenue streams for their companies.

Previously, he was the Regional Director of the University of Kansas Small Business Development Center. In his SBDC career, Curt consulted individually with over 1000 small business owners.

After graduating summa cum laude with a business marketing degree from Washburn University, Curt worked for a medical manufacturing company. He became the Vice President of Sales and Marketing and helped the owner develop the business (revenues up over 1000% in 13 years) and successfully sell it to one of its major customers.

Curt is a graduate from the Coach U training program, the largest, most comprehensive educational program for professional success coaches, and is a member of the International Coaching Federation, Sales and Marketing Executives, and the American Marketing Association. Curt is also a certified instructor for the Ewing Marion Kaufmann Foundation's FastTrac® entrepreneurial program.

Curt has written numerous articles pertaining to marketing and entrepreneurship and is the author of the book, *CUSTOMER PILLARS*: Nine foundational business building principles which dictate the revenue and profitability progress of every successful company.

Curt lives in Topeka, Kansas with his wife, Summer. He can be reached at curt@ strivecoaching.com.